Endorsements

Beth Olson is a great friend of mine. I know her well. She is one of the most energetic, determined, creative persons I know. She grew up as a missionary kid. In her new book, you can follow a life story of difficult decisions she made in following her passion: knowing God intimately. You'll also learn how to apply what she learned for practical use in your own journey. Her challenges to you at the end of each chapter will bless and instruct you. They will call forth the gold God has put in your own life. I wish the world had more than just one Beth Olson in it. Also, follow her on her blog, bethlolson.com/blog for further fresh insights.

Bob L. Phillips
Former Pastor with David Wilkerson at
Times Square Church
Current Teaching Pastor at Heartland Church and
Director of Academy for Cultural Transformation

This book is about an ordinary girl, following an extraordinary God, and in turn discovering an extraordinary life. I love how Beth shows the call of God truly is generational. We hear how her parents' obedience shaped her own, and how that impact continues on in the lives of her children. Not content to merely share her story, she challenges us all to discover our own. I love her encouragement to all of us to discover what "brand" we are. Read it and be entertained. But more importantly, read it and be provoked to embark upon your personal extraordinary life.

David L. Olson, Senior Pastor
Heartland Church, Ankeny, Iowa

I am so honored to endorse Beth Olson's book entitled, *Diary of a Missionary Kid.* Her journey as a missionary's daughter challenges each of us to embrace the road we have been given allowing God to mold and shape us into His image for His purposes. Each chapter reflects Beth's encounter with missionary life and how its joys and struggles impact and reflect in her life today. Her stories will make you laugh and cry as they stimulate and encourage you to run your race for His Glory as Beth continues to do. Having known Beth since she was a teenager, I can say that she has truly lived a life devoted to the One Whom she loves. This is a must read.

Julaine Christensen, Director and Senior Leader
The Omaha HUB and Current Fire Ministries
Omaha, NE

Does your heart yearn for a deeper and more astonished relationship with Jesus? He longs for one with you as well! *Diary of a Missionary Kid* by Beth Olson is a must read for anyone who desires to live a wide-eyed adventure with God. The journey of Beth Olson is the ripe fruit of a life courageously and honestly lived. It is an honor to endorse this remarkable read.

Leif Hetland
Founder and President, Global Mission Awareness
Author of *Seeing Through Heaven's Eyes*

Beth L Olson

Diary of a Missionary Kid

Filled with Strategy to Unlock Your Destiny

Beth L. Olson

Copyright © 2016 Beth L. Olson

ISBN-13: 978-1523745616
ISBN-10: 1523745614

Beth L Olson

Dedication

I would like to dedicate this book to my family:

My grandparents, who have all passed on to glory

My mom and dad, Leanne & Ray Goff

My husband, Christopher

My four children, Judah, Levi, Elijah, and Zoe

My brother, Jeffrey

My wonderful in-laws, Faye & Jim Olson

All of my aunts, uncles, cousins, brothers and sisters-in-laws, nieces, and nephews

My future grandkids

My spiritual parents, Bob & Sherry Phillips

My spiritual kids present and future

Beth L Olson

Table of Contents

Foreword

On April 29, 1977, God blessed my husband and me with a beautiful baby girl who would bring more joy to our lives than we could have ever dreamed possible. That beautiful baby girl would become the author this book, *Diary of a Missionary Kid*.

As far back as I can remember, I have always dreamed of being a missionary. When missionaries would come to our church in Louisiana, I would sit on the edge of the pew listening intently to every word spoken. I was mesmerized by every slide shown of their work around the world. All I could think was, *When I grow up I want to be a missionary.*

In September 1976, during a revival service at our church, I came to realize that as a "good Southern Baptist woman" I had never truly surrendered my life to Christ. I was on the road to hell. Needless to say, I got gloriously saved that very day. I followed in obedience with Baptism two nights later. A couple of weeks later I received some of the best news I would ever hear: I was pregnant with our first child. I do not believe it was an accident that when I was born again and baptized, Beth was in my womb. It only makes sense that the same passion for missions that was on my heart and in my spirit would be passed on to my daughter.

As you journey through Beth's book, don't just read it, but let it read you! From the very first page your heart will be captivated by her life story. Imagine with Beth being held-up with guns by the Mexican Mafia in the desert, being seasick on a YWAM Mercy Ship in the South Pacific, or experiencing the "surprised" moment when God told her who she would marry. As you read you will go through various emotions. You will be mesmerized, captivated, stunned, as well as challenged.

Ray and I couldn't be more proud of our "little girl" who has grown into such an amazing wife, mother, and woman of God.

Leanne Goff, Senior Pastor
Family of Faith Community Church, Newark, Ohio
Founder and President of Leanne Goff Ministries

To My Dear Family

We are running the race of life together, and I love each one of you. God has a destiny for our family, and I am passionately praying that every single one of us will live out our full potential for His kingdom and glory!

It would break my heart for any one of you to miss out on the wonderful adventures that God has prepared for you. I am cheering each of you on as you live His dream for your life!

A special thanks to Kristi Alhussaini who helped me to realize that I have a story worth telling.

Beth L Olson

Prologue

I stood with tears rolling down my cheeks. The thought of the pain of dying was more than I could bear. I was scared, gripped with the fear of the unknown. It was 1986. I was only eight years old.

There I was holding hands with my mom as our family stood in the middle of the Mexican desert while Mafia men with machine guns held us at gunpoint. At the time we had no idea who these men were or what they wanted with us.

As we stood waiting, we prayed. We were with a group of people from Youth with a Mission on a two-month outreach tour of Mexico. Team members began to kneel next to cactus plants as they sang to the Lord and repented of anything they could possibly think of to repent for.

I really can't say how long we waited in the dirt because when you live through something like that, time seems to lose all sense of reality. I guess it was thirty minutes to an hour later when the men decided we were not worth their time, piled into their cars, and sped off.

Relief and thanksgiving rushed over us. God had saved the day and rescued His children from a premature death.

This is by far the most dramatic memory from my childhood. You may think that after an event like this, I would be dead set against the idea of anyone raising their kids on the mission field, but that line of thinking could not be farther from the truth.

I am so thankful that missionaries raised me. My life has been full of adventure, and I have learned the faithfulness of God first hand.

Please join me as I share some of my adventures with you. I hope you will be inspired to embark on an adventure yourself.

Like the sun that rises every day,
You are so faithful. Lord, You are faithful.
Like the rain that You send,
And every breath that I breathe,
You are so faithful, Lord

Like the rose that comes alive every spring,
You are so faithful. Lord, You are faithful.
Like the life that You give,
to every beat of my heart,
You are so faithful, Lord.

I see the cross and the price You had to pay,
I see the blood that washed my sins away.

In the midst of the storm
through the wind and the waves,
You'll still be faithful, You'll still be faithful,
When the stars refuse to shine and time is no more,
You'll still be faithful,
You'll still be faithful, Lord.

(You Are So Faithful by Bob Fitts)

Beth L Olson

Chapter 1

Dorm 3

The call to ministry is often multi-generational. My great grandfather was a fiery Baptist preacher. He spent his life preaching hellfire and brimstone sermons in a little country church. While his ministry style was different from what we operate in today, it has become apparent that my mom inherited a call to ministry from him.

> The call to ministry is often multi-generational.

My mom's mom, known to me as Granny, used to take her kids to church on Sunday mornings, as it was part of the culture in the Deep South where they lived. Granny was a praying woman who loved Jesus and read her Bible regularly.

Before my mom ever gave her life to the Lord, she remembers being mesmerized by the slide shows that visiting missionaries would share with her church. The testimonies the missionaries shared awakened in her young heart a call to the nations.

My Granny worked for various airlines for about thirty years. One of the perks of her job was that she was able to take her family flying standby on trips all over the world. These trips served to stir my mom's adventurous spirit while giving her valuable practice in international traveling.

When I was in first grade my parents went on their very first mission trip to Honduras, Central America, with a small group from our Baptist church in Kenner, Louisiana. Central America was torn apart by civil war at the time. The area where they went was literally a war zone.

That did not slow them down. Before the trip, they went to meetings with the other team members to prepare as much as possible. They also sold all of our living room and dining room furniture, plus MY bedroom furniture to pay for their trip!

I felt very sad to be left at home because I was very attached to my parents. One thing my parents were awesome at was finding someone to stay with my brother and me whom we truly felt comfortable with.

At the time of this first trip, I was attending the private school at our Baptist church. My teacher was actually the one who stayed with my brother and me. That was a wonderful arrangement which I still remember feeling happy about because I really liked my teacher.

At that time my parents spoke almost no Spanish. To reach out to people they would go out to the market place and town square and hand out little pieces of paper called tracts with the saving message of Christ written on them in Spanish. They would point to the different lines on the tract to have the person read each point. Then they would pray with the person using their very limited Spanish skills.

They also used record players made out of cardboard to share the message. They used a pencil to turn the record manually so that the Spanish-speaking people could hear a prerecorded message in their own language.

Believe it or not, these methods actually worked. Many people came to the Lord in spite of the language barrier.

One of the most challenging parts of market ministry was the overwhelming stench of the place. At the time Honduras was the poorest nation in Central America. It was completely normal for people to urinate and otherwise relieve themselves in the streets. There was also rotting fruit, vegetables, and meat hanging in the marketplace.

The team leader, Leo, was determined to help my mom get past the putrid smells. He would grab her hand and say, "Get ready. Hold your breath." Then he would drag her from one side of the market to the other. When they got through to the other side he would say, "Take a deep breath." Then he would grab her hand and pull her through again. He did this over and over again until mom could be in the market without feeling like she was going to puke.

Leo became a spiritual father to our family in our journey into the missionary life. He was patient and kind, and God used him to push our family into our destiny.

When mom and dad got home from that first trip they had to wait a week to get their pictures back from being developed. After they got the pictures my mom would just sit on the edge of her bed looking at them and weeping. When they would look at the pictures, it was like they could see every person in them sitting right in front of them.

Soon after that first trip my mom made enough money from selling real estate to replace all of the furniture they had sold to pay for the trip. Even so, there was no turning back to a normal American lifestyle after what they had experienced during their time in Honduras.

While in Honduras mom and dad met a sweet little girl named Christiana. They spent some time trying to adopt her when they got home, but it never worked out. So, they moved full force toward adopting the nations.

The search for the right path into full time missions was set in motion. Mom went on two more trips to Honduras while dad stayed home with us kids and continued to work at his well-paying, secure job at a grain elevator on the Mississippi River. He was wrestling with God about whether it was wise for him to leave the security that his job gave our family and go into full time missions work.

After a couple of years, mom and dad went on another trip to Honduras. While on that trip, my dad spent a whole night pacing the hotel room floor as he wrestled with God over the call to missions.

Shortly after returning home, dad's company laid him off because there had been a downturn in the economy. The security barrier was removed. We had a big yard sale where we sold the majority of our possessions.

Mom and dad wanted to serve in Honduras, but because of the dangerous civil war, they did not want to strike out on their own. They wanted to get much needed missionary training and support.

The Goff Family

They prayed and asked God to lead them. He connected them to new friends who told them about Youth With a Mission. It was a perfect fit for us.

As a family of four we left our home in the New Orleans, Louisiana area and joined Youth with a Mission (YWAM) in Lindale, Texas for their Discipleship Training School (DTS).

For three months, mom and dad attended classes while my brother Jeffrey attended a small kindergarten on the mission base, and I was homeschooled with a few other kids by a staff member's wife.

During those three months we lived in "Dorm 3" with a couple other families and a bunch of singles. My brother and I had a room that we shared, and mom and dad lived across the hallway.

It was a fun environment to be in. I remember lying in bed at night listening to music and feeling happy. My biggest worry at the time was that I would fall out of my top bunk in the middle of the night because it had no railing.

My dad would tuck the edge of my blanket under the mattress at night to help me feel less worried about it. I honestly have no idea why I thought that would help, but I never fell out of bed. Years later it dawned on me that I had never fallen out of a regular bed, so there was no reason why I would have been prone to falling out of a bed that just happened to be a bit higher up in the air.

In Dorm 3 we had a shared kitchen that we used mostly for breakfast. Lunch and dinner meals were eaten at the base cafeteria along with the rest of the people on the ministry base. A special treat my dad would occasionally give us was to let my brother and I share a can of Mt. Dew, which he would buy from the coke machine for a quarter.

The cafeteria was connected to a gymnasium. There was also another room in the same building that had old video arcade style games like Pac-Man and Donkey Kong. One day my brother ran into the arcade room, tripped over a power cord, hit his head on the edge of a game table, and split his forehead open. My parents had to rush him to a nearby town where he got several stitches. Boys will be boys, missionary kid or not.

The class that my parents were in had 118 students from all over the world. Part of the missionary training was a class called "Father Heart of God."

During this class, God did a deep healing work in my mom's heart. Her biological father had abandoned her at birth, and she had a lot of pain and bitterness deep inside her heart because of it. She learned about the need to forgive and found great freedom as she made the choice to let the pain go. Read all about it in my mom's book *A Christian Life Without Father God.*

After the three months of classroom time came to a close, we got our immunizations, picked up our bottles of malaria pills, and packed our bags.

A large group of the students from the school packed up and piled into a big yellow school bus to head to Guatemala.

As we traveled from city to city my brother and I did our schoolwork on the bus. We would study, and when we were ready for a nap my dad would lift us into the overhead luggage racks so we could stretch out.

We drove through Southern Texas and Mexico, camping along the way. We spent our nights in tents sleeping in sleeping bags.

> When we were ready for a nap my dad would lift us into the overhead luggage racks so we could stretch out.

Sometimes we camped on the beach in tents or slept in hammocks. The beaches had black sand from volcanic ash. It was wonderful to hear the sound of the waves crashing against the shore all night long. In the mornings iguanas would be sitting on rocks all around us.

My brother got very sick while we were camping on the beach, and mom had to wash his sleeping bag out in the ocean several times. I can't imagine how she managed to do it without getting it full of sand.

So many of the people on the team were sick. Someone suggested that raw coconut milk would help soothe stomachs. The guys managed to get some coconuts down from the trees by shaking the trees or climbing them. They chopped off the tops of the coconuts with a machete. I did not care for the taste of the milk much, but it seemed to help the ones who were sick.

Another interesting drink was Coca Cola in a bag. Coke was sold in glass bottles and it cost a lot more to buy it if you didn't have an empty bottle to turn in for recycling. To avoid having to sell a bottle, the shop keepers would pour the coke into a plastic sandwich bag, stick a straw in it, and hand it over. This was a great solution as long as you planned to drink the whole thing at once. You couldn't really set it somewhere and drink it later.

I distinctly remember one place that we stayed. Our family actually had a solid shelter to live in for ten days. We lived in a concrete room with openings for a door and windows. There was no actual door or windows in the openings, but that didn't matter much. We hung sheets over the doors for a little privacy.

We had an outhouse with a real toilet, which had to be flushed by pouring a bucket of water into the bowl. The buckets of water had to be hauled from the well a few blocks away.

The guys on the team would go to the well in the middle of the day to haul all of the day's water supply. They could not go in the mornings because all of the women from the village took their baths at the well in the mornings, and the men had their turn in the evenings.

It was an interesting experience bathing at a well along with a whole village. I guess I am just glad I was still a little kid and not overly shy about being modest.

The women not only used the mornings to bathe at the well, they also washed all of their family's clothes by hand at the same time.

There was a huge garbage pile about twenty steps from the door of our temporary home. God only knows what kinds of critters were living in that mound. We used to joke about the dogs chasing the cats that were chasing the rats. Throw chickens and a noisy rooster in the mix and you start to get the picture.

> We used to joke about the dogs chasing the cats that were chasing the rats. Throw chickens and a noisy rooster in the mix and you start to get the picture.

There was also a turkey tied up outside our room. It would gobble all throughout the night. To make matters even more interesting, there was an old stove in our room that rats liked to hide in. We could hear them scurrying around in the stove all night.

None of these things bothered me much. I considered them a normal part of life. The one thing that bothered me was my weekly malaria pill. The malaria pills at that time were extremely bitter. Even if you could swallow the pill very quickly and chase it with something that had a good flavor, it would still gag you. The pills were bitter, bitter, bitter!

To make matters worse, I just could not figure out how to swallow a pill. I think I have a very strong gag reflex. Every week my parents would have to smash up the pill and mix it with sugar, peanut butter, or anything they could find and force feed it to me. I can honestly still remember the taste of those pills all these years later. I am happy to say that at least I never caught malaria.

I struggled a lot with meal times as a child. I was a very picky eater, which was unfortunate for me. Sometimes I just didn't eat. I remember refusing to eat canned ravioli. It was the only thing available that day, and I was so hungry. I just couldn't bring myself to choke it down no matter how much my stomach growled.

At long last we arrived at our destination in Guatemala. We set up our tents at the YWAM base in Guatemala City. Because I was so young at the time I do not have many memories of the outreaches that our group did. I remember more of the day-to-day activities.

The YWAM base we stayed at was a former mansion and had a large swimming pool. On the floor of the pool there was a Star of David made out of bright blue pieces of ceramic tile. We thought that was so cool. The weather was really too cold for swimming, but we just had to try that pool out. Boy, were we cold!

The base had two German Shepherd guard dogs named Shilo and Terry that roamed the property at nighttime. They were trained to attack anyone who spoke Spanish. We had to be very careful to only speak English in our sleepiness when we needed to leave our tents in the middle of the night to use the bathroom.

The bathrooms were about thirty yards away from our tents. We were told to walk slowly with our hands at our sides so the dogs could sniff them.

Most days my dad wore mime makeup and my mom dressed up as a clown as we went out to the streets and shared about Jesus. Crowds of people would stop to check out the crazy Americans. We sang songs that we memorized in Spanish and did puppet shows for the kids. We handed out Gospel tracts to the adults and stickers to the kids.

Most of the kids had never seen a sticker ever before. They would try to hide them by sticking them to their skin under their shirts so they could come back for more. You could see them over to the side lifting up their shirts to show their friends how many stickers they had stuck to their backs and stomachs.

One time we had to get on the bus as fast as we could because the kids were mobbing us for stickers. As we slowly drove out of the crowd, kids were hanging all over the bus trying to get to us. Can you imagine being that desperate for a simple sticker?

Some of my favorite outreach times were the times that we visited orphanages. We would sing songs and do puppet shows and then just play with the kids.

One orphanage we visited was situated near a volcano that had smoke blowing from its top. There were a lot of kids at this orphanage and to clean them up they would strip them, line them up, and spray them down with a water hose. The kids didn't seem to mind it one bit.

After spending several weeks at the YWAM base in Guatemala, we journeyed back to Texas.

As we traveled on the bus day after day, the team started to run low on money. The money that remained had to be saved to buy gas for the bus. We had to drive out of Guatemala, five days through Mexico, and one more day through Texas.

Apparently whoever was in charge of meals had not planned the menus out very well. The adults went without eating for five days, but they did feed us kids the little that they had: peanut butter and jelly on corn tortillas! Haha, I don't remember it being too bad. I liked it better than canned ravioli for sure.

After the five days of mandatory fasting for the adults, our team ministered at a church. The church took up an offering for us, which allowed us to purchase food for the rest of the trip home.

Our first portion of missionary training was complete. We moved back to Louisiana for several months to focus on raising funds so we could return to Texas for the second phase of training.

> We needed to learn how to fit in culturally in whatever setting we found ourselves.

We spent time visiting friends and family, which included a few days at Granny's house. Now, in many countries the sewage systems are not built to handle toilet paper. Jeffrey and I were well trained to always put our toilet paper in the trash can instead of flushing it. Granny did not care for that! She told my mom to make us stop doing that at her house. We needed to learn how to fit in culturally in whatever setting we found ourselves.

Making a friend at an orphanage

Strategy to Unlock Your Destiny

Family Callings

Take some time to research your family history. Maybe you have parents or grandparents who were involved in something great.

If when you go back only one or two generations you don't find spiritual legacy, go back further.

There is sure to be a great grandparent along your line who loved God and had a genuine connection with Him.

God may also bring one or more spiritual parents into your life. As you lean your heart into theirs, spiritual inheritance can be passed on to you.

If you still can't find anyone, go all the way back to Father Abraham. You have an inheritance even through him.

God gave Himself to Abraham as his reward and shield. Then He told told Abraham that his children would be as many as the stars he could see in the sky.

You are one of those kids. That means that you have access to Abraham's inheritance. God is YOUR reward and shield.

In fact, you can go back even further than Father Abraham.

Your Father God has been longing to know you and to see your destiny unfold since before the earth was even created.

Latching onto your inheritance from Father God is your ultimate claim. He owns EVERYTHING, and He can't wait to share it with you.

Get into the Bible and read all about what God has prepared for you. His Word is your guide book. Ask Holy Spirit to help you as you read. You may not understand much at first, but don't give up. Even if your mind doesn't understand, your spirit will be receiving much needed nutrients.

You may find reading the Bible to be boring at times, but if you don't give up you will eventually develop a deep love for God's Word.

Destiny key: Make sure you track down your parent's stories because they are doorways into your potential. You can pull on them to receive inheritance.

Chapter 2

Running Full Force Ahead

Before we knew it we were back at Twin Oaks Ranch in Lindale, Texas, for my parents' School of Evangelism (SOE) training with YWAM. After three months of training time, we would head out for an outreach tour of Mexico.

We lived in Dorm 5 for three months. I did a lot of normal childhood type things while we lived there. I learned to ride my bike, learned how to play chess, and worked very hard on memorizing my times tables.

I attended 3rd grade at a Christian school for those three months. I really enjoyed spending time with the other kids. After lunch we had recess time. We would save our plastic sandwich bags and use them to collect grasshoppers. I really enjoyed the grasshopper hunts.

If it happened to be muddy out, the teacher would make us take our shoes off before we came back into class. I always hoped my shoes were dirty! I loved not having to wear shoes to class.

I also got to play the part of an angel in the school's Christmas play. I got to wear a pretty costume.

School Christmas Play

Before we knew it, it was time to head out for outreach again. This time we rode in a 1948 Streamline bus. It was the kind you see in old movies. It was a little more comfortable than the school bus we used for our

DTS outreach. It had reclining seats, which made the ride a little easier.

Every few hours the bus would make a stop so we could go to the bathroom either behind a cactus in the desert or at a less than spotless gas station bathroom. The desert pit stops were preferable. No matter where the pit stop location was, it was always B.Y.O.T.P. (Bring your own toilet paper.)

Youth With a Mission is the largest missions organization in the world. From top to bottom no one receives a paycheck. Volunteers pay a small amount each month to cover their living costs while they serve. Operating on a shoestring budget meant that the buses we used were in far from perfect condition. Breaking down on the side of the road was a normal occurrence.

One time the bus's fan came loose, flew into the radiator, and tore it up. We stayed in a small hotel in the desert while a couple of our guys traveled to a town eight hours away to get the radiator fixed.

It was very cold. I remember taking a cold shower and having my hair washed in what felt like ice cubes. We were freezing in the hotel room. We decided to sleep on the bus the second night.

While the guys were away, others worked on repairing the bus's fan. They set it on a huge rock and proceeded to beat it back into shape with a rock. Necessity is the mother of invention.

Once the bus was ready to go we hit the road again. We had to stop every few miles to get water from water holes and streams so we could use it to cool down the radiator.

We did not make it very far before the bus broke down again. This time the drive shaft just fell out. It had fifteen bolts holding it in place, but they all just fell out.

It was on this trip that we had our run in with the Mexican mafia. We were on the side of the road in the desert when three carloads of men with machine guns zoomed up to our bus.

One car parked in front of the bus and the other two directly behind it. They demanded that everyone get off the bus, and that our leaders show them our paperwork without delay.

I stood with my parents while tears rolled down my cheeks. The thought of the pain of dying was more than I could bear. I was scared, gripped with the fear of the unknown.

There I was holding hands with my mom as our family stood in the middle of the Mexican desert while Mafia men with machine guns held us at gunpoint. At the time we had no idea who these men were or what they wanted with us.

> The thought of the pain of dying was more than I could bear.

One of the team translators told our team leader that the men wanted to see our papers right away.

Our leader said, "Okay, just a minute."

The translator responded, "No, you don't understand, they want them NOW!"

As we stood waiting, we prayed. Team members began to kneel next to cactus plants as they sang to the Lord and repented of anything they could possibly think to repent for.

I really can't say how long we stood there because, when you live through something like that, time seems to lose all sense of reality. I guess it was thirty minutes to an hour later that the men decided we were not worth their time, piled back into their cars, and sped off.

After catching our breath and thanking the Lord, we loaded back onto the bus and headed towards Fresnillo, Mexico. There we spent ten days ministering through drama and puppet shows while we processed all that had happened on the side of the road.

We arrived in Mexico City only months after a massive 8.0 earthquake had killed 5,000 people and collapsed over 400 buildings. There was a huge hospital building that YWAM was using as a base. YWAMers from all over the world were coming and going to this base all the time. There were about three hundred of us living there together.

Our family shared a room with a newlywed couple from our team. We hung up a bed sheet as a divider in the middle of the room so that we could have the most basic amount of privacy.

It was very cold in Mexico City at the time of our visit. The building was still under construction; about 80% completed, and had no hot water. Every week or two we would walk over to the public "baños" (baths) and take a hot shower. That was a real treat.

We carried our laundry with us so mom could wash it in the hot water. I guess she learned this particular kind of multi-tasking from our time bathing at the well.

Granny came to visit us while we were in Mexico City. She stayed in a very nice hotel, and we took advantage of the hot water there too!

Granny also took us to see the pyramids. We climbed the Pyramid of the Sun, which is the third largest pyramid in the world. We decided to take in the Pyramid of the Moon from ground level. Climbing one pyramid was adventure enough.

> We climbed the Pyramid of the Sun, which is the third largest pyramid in the world.

At the beginning of our stay in Mexico City we rode the subways for transportation. The subways turned out to be very dangerous. Some of our people had jewelry, wallets, and important travel documents stolen. Some of the women were man handled. The subways were so crowded that it was really impossible to defend yourself.

We quickly gave up on underground travel and began to walk to most of the places we had to go. The sidewalks were not level and frequently had potholes. My dad would always say, "Watch where you're walking."

More than ten years later I realized that I had developed a strong habit of looking at the ground when I walk. I thought that was funny. I still have to remind myself to look up and take in the sights when I walk.

I remember making tortillas by hand with the women in Mexico. I really enjoyed that. Most of all I enjoyed spending time with people. By this time, I was very used to living in community.

Strategy to Unlock Your Destiny

Ready, Set, Go!

Do you have big dreams but don't know where to start? Maybe you lack the confidence that you will be successful.

You really have to start somewhere. It is like the old question. How do you eat an elephant? One bite at a time.

When people ask my husband how he learned to speak Spanish he often responds, "You have to speak bad Spanish before you can speak good Spanish."

His desire to speak other languages is much greater than his desire to not look foolish. This thinking has served him well.

Pride is sometimes what stops us from trying. We don't like to look silly in front of other people, but you simply cannot be perfect at something the first time you do it.

You have to be willing to try and to fail. Fear of looking like a fool is pride.

God resists the proud, but gives grace to the humble. (James 4:6)

This is something that I personally struggle with. I much prefer to do everything as "perfectly" as I can the first time around.

I spend hours studying and researching a thing before I do it. I think there is wisdom in preparing well, but at some point you have to stop preparing and move forward.

I have to remind myself that if I am willing to humble myself and take a step forward, grace will come to me.

You have to start somewhere. We have to get right up to the starting line and take that first step.

No one is born knowing how to walk gracefully. You literally have to take baby steps. Take some baby steps towards fulfilling your destiny today.

Destiny key: Everything worth doing is worth doing poorly....at the beginning.

Sometimes life feels like you're pushing against a brick wall. It can be very frustrating when you have things in your heart to accomplish; you work hard and get smacked with what feels like strong resistance.

It reminds me of those blocking sleds they use in football practice. The athletes push with all their might only to get minimal movement.

Sometimes to get something off the ground you have to push. Pushing is hard, painful work, but the fact that it is time to push means that something awesome is about to break forth.

When I was in labor with my first son, there was a distinct moment when the pain became so strong, that I just wanted to stop, climb out of the hospital bed, and go home. I had been waiting for that day with all of my heart for nine months, honestly for my whole life. Even so, when the pain became overwhelming, I just wanted to "stick a pin in it" and try again another day.

Turn back the clock another 23 years. When my mom was ready to give birth to me something crazy happened. When the time to push came, her doctor instructed the nurses to hold her off for what turned out to be several hours.

This delay caused physical damage to my mom. She had to have follow-up surgery and ended up only being able to bear two children when she would have liked to have had more.

Sometimes you just have to push! Quitting is not an option, and delay is dangerous.

This is the moment when the resistance actually works for you. Great breakthrough is imminent if you keep pressing forward.

Whenever a woman is in labor she has pain, because her hour has come; but when she gives birth to the child, she no longer remembers the anguish because of the joy that a child has been born into the world. (John 16:21)

Our biggest breakthroughs come when we keep pushing.

Behold, I will do something new, now it will spring forth; Will you not be aware of it? I will even make a roadway in the wilderness, rivers in the desert. (Isaiah 43:19)

Please do not take this as permission to push against God or against your leaders in a rebellious way. That is definitely not what I am suggesting. If you push too early, you will birth a preemie and go through a lot of added stress.

Chapter 3

Home is Wherever You Can Drive To

After School of Evangelism our family moved to New Orleans to serve at the YWAM base. There we lived in a duplex shotgun house. A shotgun house is a house where all the rooms are lined up so that you could shoot a bullet from the front door and it would pass through every room in the house and go right out the back door.

Our next-door neighbors were punk rockers who had brightly colored Mohawks. It was quite a different experience from the Latin culture we had grown accustomed to. The neighborhood we lived in was very dangerous. We could not keep anything, not even a plant, on our porch without someone stealing it.

Mom and dad were busy doing ministry stuff while we kids just did normal kid stuff. We played with the neighbor kids on the other side of our house, whose parents were also with YWAM. We played board games, and I learned to cross-stitch.

My mom decided to give me a perm one day. Hair permanents were very stylish at the time. I had very fine, straight hair, so she decided to switch it up a bit. When she got it all done I went outside to show my dad. As soon as I came back into the house I looked in the mirror and saw that all the curl had fallen right out. The extreme humidity in the New Orleans air made my fine hair go completely flat. So much for that idea!

> Our next-door neighbors were punk rockers with brightly colored Mohawks.

One day my brother and his friend decided it would be fun to pile cushions on the floor and jump off the top of the bunk bed onto the soft cushions. It was all fun and games until Jeffrey decided to jump with his tongue sticking out. As he jumped his knee came up and slammed into his chin causing him to bite a big hole in his tongue. There was blood everywhere, but the doctor said he would not put stitches in a tongue unless it was literally falling off.

I remember him sitting at our kitchen table with a Popsicle in his mouth to help reduce the pain and swelling. He still has a big scar on his tongue to this day.

After our time in New Orleans we loaded up our van and a trailer and headed back to the YWAM base in Guatemala for six months. It takes about a week to drive from Louisiana or Texas to Guatemala, but that could not deter us. Wherever God said, "Go," we just went.

It was peaceful living in Guatemala. We had our own two-bedroom apartment with a bathroom. That was a big step up from the tent home we lived in the first time we were there. We got to spend a lot of quality time as a family. I really enjoyed playing Monopoly and Bible Trivia all together.

> Wherever God said, "Go,"
> we just went.

Occasionally for a treat mom would buy a two-liter of grape or orange Fanta and put it in the freezer until it got really slushy. It tasted delicious. Once in a great while we would drive to McDonalds and have an ice cream sundae.

Sometimes my brother and I would go down to the cafeteria early to help swat flies. There is something wonderful about swatting a little pest: the flies, not my brother!

There was a little Indian man who did maintenance work around the property. We used to go out behind the cafeteria and watch him make cement tables and benches. He would mix together concrete, sand, and water with a shovel and put it into molds to harden. Our Spanish was limited, but we would try to talk with him anyway.

We could not get through our time in Guatemala without my brother getting banged up a bit more. We both had bikes, but for some reason he had it in his head that he wanted to ride my bike. I was dead set against the idea. I loved that pink bike with the banana seat so much. My parents finally convinced me to let him. Right away he went out and got into a wreck!

While the bike was fine, Jeffrey did not get off so easily. He hit his head on the brick road and was very disoriented for a few hours. When he finally came around he told us that he had wanted to see what it would be like to ride with his eyes closed. Boys!

During our time in Guatemala, my parents came across a baby girl whose mother was giving her up for adoption. We were all set to take her, but on the morning we were to pick her up, we got a call that the mother had changed her mind and given her to another family. It was painful, but God knew best, as He always does.

At the close of our time in Guatemala we decided to drive a bit further south to visit friends who were missionaries in San Salvador, El Salvador.

It was a very dangerous journey to make. There was a lot of unrest in Central America at the time.

As we traveled, we drove past rows of army tanks. We passed by a hospital with wounded soldiers sitting outside. Some of them were bandaged, and some were missing limbs.

> The windows of the apartment that we stayed in would rattle at night from the bombs going off in the distance.

It was very normal to see guards armed with machine guns everywhere we went. The windows of the apartment that we stayed in rattled at night because of the bombs going off in the distance. The day before we arrived some signs were blown up right across the street from the apartment building.

The mom of the family we stayed with made the best chocolate chip cookies though, and the family had kids for us to play with. That was all I needed. I wasn't worried about anything that was going on outside of the apartment.

I had my ninth birthday in El Salvador. I had a cake with nine candles, and I was very happy.

9th Birthday in San Salvador

After a couple of weeks, we loaded up our van and trailer to head back to Louisiana. On the way there we stopped to visit some YWAM friends in Conroe, Texas.

Their church, The Worship Center, was having Vacation Bible School that week. They had a lot more kids show up than what they had planned for, so my mom and dad decided to stay for the week to help. We all very quickly felt a strong connection to that church so we ended up staying there for five years.

I would say that we had a bit more stability in our lives during those five years. We developed strong friendships with a lot of wonderful people.

Jeffrey and I attended a small private school called Calvary Baptist School. It was a wonderful place to be. I have often wished for a school like it to send my own kids to.

Every Friday of our five years at that school we had chapel day. We always sang a scripture song from Isaiah 40:31:

They that wait upon the Lord,
Will renew their strength,
They will rise up with wings like eagles,
They will run and not grow weary,
They will walk and not faint,
Teach me Lord,
Oh, teach me Lord,
To Wait

This song was something that I sang out of habit and duty, but I now realize that God took it for real. The words and the tune of that song are life to me now. I have learned that real strength and peace come to my soul when I take time to quietly wait on the Lord.

> I have learned that real strength and peace come to my soul when I take time to quietly wait on the Lord.

One summer we went to a YMCA day camp. Jeffrey was playing a game of tag that he and his friends called "Frankenstein" when he fell from some monkey bars and broke both of the bones in his arm completely through. I was so worried about him. There was a lot of drama as a fire truck, police car, and ambulance all came racing into the park. They loaded Jeffrey into the back of the ambulance and put me in the front. Then they took us both to the hospital where our parents met us. Jeffrey had to have surgery, and he wore a blue cast for several weeks. We all had a good laugh in the midst of the stressful situation when we found out that the anesthesiologist's name was Dr. BoBo.

Jeffrey was always the thrill seeking, roller coaster loving type, while I much preferred to be at home reading a good book.

It is a wonder that he didn't get banged up more often than he did since he used to ride his skateboard while holding onto the back of the delivery trucks that came through our neighborhood.

Every six to eight months our family would load up a group of people from our church into a rented RV and drive overnight for a long weekend in Reynosa, Mexico. Over the course of those five years our teams helped to build a four story brick orphanage dedicated to the children of the singer Keith Green. Keith and his two young children passed away in a plane crash in 1982.

Before the plane crash, Keith's little boy Josiah would pray every night that the little girls and boys who slept on the streets in Mexico would have a place to live. Keith's wife Melody decided to use the money that was given in their honor to build the three-story orphanage.

It was our honor to be a part of the building process. The first time we went down to help, our guys dug the holes for the foundation of the building. It was so rewarding to see the progress over the years. Eventually we were able to stay in the completed building with the kids that were being cared for.

When I was thirteen years old we rented an apartment in Reynosa just minutes away from the orphanage. We lived in the apartment for the summer. The rest of the year we used it to house the groups from Texas that continued to help at the orphanage every few weeks.

It was extremely hot and dusty in Reynosa. Every morning my mom would sweep and mop the apartment while I dusted it. Late morning, we would all head over to the orphanage to spend time with the kids and help out however we could.

I learned a lot of Spanish while spending time at the orphanage. I was like a sponge soaking everything up.

> I seriously wanted to dye my hair black. I had no idea how ridiculous that would have looked.

I really wanted the freedom to be able to walk from our house to the orphanage alone, but my parents said that it was not safe for me. My hair was blonde, and I stood out in the crowd wherever we went. I seriously wanted to dye my hair black. I had no idea how ridiculous that would have looked.

The majority of the kids at the orphanage were not true orphans in that they still had families. Their families could not afford to take care of them so they handed them over to those who were willing to help. Sometimes the families would visit the kids. It was sad that most of the kids could not be adopted into permanent homes.

There was one young toddler name Carlitos that our family fell in love with. My parents tried to adopt him, but it just didn't work out. Sometimes I still wonder where he is and how he is doing.

I especially loved spending time in the babies' room. I would spend hours holding the abandoned babies. It was an added perk that the nursery was equipped with more fans than any other room.

Lice were an occupational hazard. Most of the kids at the public schools had lice, which made for a constant battle for the kids at the orphanage. My mom became an expert in lice eradication. I am lucky that she never gave up and chopped off all of my hair.

> My mom became an expert in lice eradication. I am lucky that she never gave up and chopped off all of my hair.

We also spent many hours helping to wash the kids' clothes. In the early days we washed the clothes by hand and hung them up to dry. Eventually a couple of washing machines were donated.

The laundry area was on the rooftop of the building. Doing laundry was great exercise because you first had to climb four flights of steps, then you had to haul baskets of wet clothes out to the clothes lines.

The piles of laundry were unending, but the hot Reynosa sunshine made line drying a very quick process. You had to be careful not to let the wet laundry touch the rooftop because the roof was covered with dust. If you happened to drop a shirt it had to go right back into the dirty clothes pile.

Many times when we had groups from Texas

helping out, the women would spend all day working in the kitchen or washing clothes while the guys did hard physical labor on the building.

In America we have wonderful tools and equipment to make work more efficient. In Mexico at that time, building was a slow process. Cement supplies had to be hauled in by wheelbarrow and then mixed by hand. Bricks were lifted four stories into the air with a simple pulley.

Washing Dishes at the Orphanage

On days that we were not working at the orphanage we would take the teams out to the streets where they would do dramas to share Jesus with the local people. The Americans would share testimonies and preach while a bilingual person translated for them.

After the street outreach we would all go back to the orphanage to play ball with the kids or blow bubbles with them.

Sometimes we did medical clinics in villages. Medical professionals from the United States would join with us to serve lines of people that would wait in the hot sun all day. One place we did a clinic at was an area where multiple families live in old train cars.

We often did outreaches where we gave away bags of beans and rice to poor families. We would spend hours scooping a few hundred pounds of beans and rice out of huge bags and repackaging them into gallon sized bags.

Our team members jokingly sang, "We bring a sack of rice with Ray (my dad) into the house of the poor," to the tune of the old song "We bring a sacrifice of praise into the house of the Lord."

I now have Mexican friends in Iowa who lived in a very poor, remote area of Mexico as children. They remember people like us coming to give food and other kinds of assistance to their neighborhood when they were young. It is amazing what a little food can do to reach a person's heart.

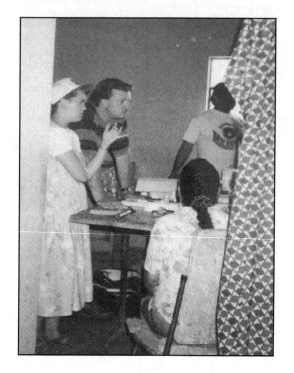

Translating at a Medical Outreach

Strategy to Unlock Your Destiny

Fuel for the Journey

My dream is for us all to dream big and go after our dreams with everything we have. Regardless of how exciting dream chasing is, life will always be full of boring moments.

We all have basic maintenance things we have to do each day. We have to clean our homes, feed our dogs, and fill our cars with gas over and over again.

Personally I find it tedious to wash my face and brush my teeth every single night. I choose to be faithful in these little things because I know that they are important in both the short and long term.

These maintenance moments are some of the basic building blocks of life.

Sometimes God leaves us in a place of boring repetition because He has us in a holding pattern. Regardless of how boring our lives may seem, people around us are watching.

There will suddenly come a moment when all of your steadiness will pay off. Your consistent choosing to have a joyful attitude in the midst of a plain, normal life will open up the door for a "wow" moment.

You never can tell when your faithfulness will open the door for you to make a forever impact in someone's life.

Let us not lose heart in doing good, for in due time we will reap if we do not grow weary. (Galatians 6:9)

It is vital to develop a deep relationship with Holy Spirit. I love Holy Spirit so much. He's just so good.

The intimate fellowship that I experience with Him is like nothing else in this life. It fills me with peace that is beyond comprehension.

I know that this is a huge part of what Jesus was talking about when He said, *the thief comes only to steal and kill and destroy; I came that they may have life, and have it abundantly.* (John 10:10)

I'm so thankful to Jesus that He went to His Father and sent Holy Spirit to us: the Spirit of Truth who teaches us everything we need to know.

The devil hates for us to experience this sweet fellowship with Holy Spirit. He whispers so many lies to keep us from this divine connection.

Some of the lies he used on me over the years were:

1. You're not hearing from God or feeling anything really spiritual. You are just making

stuff up.

2. You're not as spiritual as other people, so you might as well serve others and not even try to have spiritual encounters.

3. If you were really spiritual, you could connect with God without using music as a crutch.

Wow! Do you see how accusing those statements are? I had to learn to recognize where the thoughts in my head were coming from.

Any thought that is accusing and keeping you from connecting with God, definitely is not from God. He greatly desires to connect with you.

What freedom! When I realized that over the years I really had been sincere in my love for God, and that He knew that and loved that about me, I started to enter into His presence in a whole new way.

Now when I spend time with the Lord, I have confidence. I know that I love Him, and He loves me.

Now I have thoughts running through my head like:

1. Holy Spirit, I love you so much. I love it when You come and spend time with me.

2. Jesus, thank you so much that I am clean, and that it is my nature to love.

3. Father, thank You that I'm Your child, and You love to give me good gifts.

Sometimes when I spend time with God, it totally just feels like I'm "putting in my time." Other times it feels like my heart is soaring.

The amazing thing is that whether I feel dry or feel like I'm flying, every moment spent leaning my heart towards God counts.

He notices every glance that you make towards Him, and it thrills Him. Every prayer you pray, goes straight to His throne whether it feels powerful in the moment or not.

Some people connect with the Lord alone in their room, some enjoy prayer walks, and others enjoy soaking in the sunrises and sunsets. Maybe you have a long commute and enjoy that time for talking with Jesus.

If you have small children, your connection point with the Lord might happen as you sing and worship while you're washing the dishes or cleaning the house.

When my kids were young, I used to pay a high school student to spend an hour with my kids a couple afternoons a week so that I could be alone in my room to recharge and connect with the Lord. It was worth every penny as it was an important investment for my whole family.

Destiny key: experiment to find out how you best connect with the Lord, and then be intentional about doing it.

The King will answer
and say to them,
"Truly I say to you,
to the extent that you did it to
one of these brothers of Mine,
even the least of them,
you did it to Me."

Matthew 25:40

Chapter 4

Never a Dull Moment

My parents were always up for anything God asked them to do. One time my dad and a friend volunteered to drive a school bus all the way from Houston, Texas to El Salvador. The bus had been donated to our missionary friends there. The drive was supposed to take a week; after which they would fly home to the Houston airport.

The trip took much longer than expected due to bus breakdowns and other delays. Almost three weeks went by without us hearing a word from dad. My mom was definitely starting to worry.

Dad finally made it home and had plenty of new crazy stories to tell us, such as when the bus broke down in San Luis Potosi, Mexico. Some pastors there housed my dad and his friend and helped them get what they needed to get back on the road to El Salvador.

It is interesting how God weaves everything together in a way only He can do. Because of the warm reception my dad received in San Luis Potosi, that city became the next point in our journey.

When I was fourteen we moved to San Luis Potosi along with a group of families from our church in Texas. We ran a YWAM style mission's school there for one year. The school was called MASH (Missions, Actions, Schooling, and Helps).

> It is interesting how God weaves
> everything together in a way
> only He can do.

I loved my life in San Luis. The city was in the mountains, which made it a very scenic place to live. The city was at a 4,000 ft. altitude, which made the climate much nicer than what I had been used to in Reynosa. The weather was just perfect.

It was not so uncommon to see fair skinned, light haired people there, so I felt like I did not stand out quite so much.

I had been planning to start ninth grade by homeschool correspondence, but at the last minute I got bit by the adventure bug and decided to go to a Mexican school instead. We boxed up my homeschool curriculum and mailed it back to the correspondence school.

I joined a class of foreign exchange students at a Catholic school called Apostolica Instituto Cervantes. Since my parents were missionaries, the school granted me a scholarship. That sealed the deal.

Every weekday I joined a few other American high school students, a guy from Germany, and a couple students from Canada for intensive Spanish language classes.

Our teacher's name was Anselmo. He taught the entire class in Spanish. If there was a word we didn't know in Spanish, he would use other Spanish words to describe it to us.

Anselmo did speak English, but it was with a very thick accent. The only time I ever heard him speak English was when he got really mad at the students. I decided I never wanted to hear him speak English again.

The exchange students I was with were all a couple years older than me. They were pretty wild and went to a lot of parties. I was able to have some good conversations with them, and I believe I had a calming effect on some of them.

Besides my three hours of Spanish class each day, I also sat in on an algebra class and a Mexican history class with the regular students. I did not learn much other than Spanish in those classes, but they made for an interesting cultural experience.

The woman who taught the history class was very out of the box. She hardly ever opened a book. She would sit Indian style on top of her desk and chain smoke cigarettes as she told the story of Mexico from memory. There was nothing boring about her class. She was a great storyteller.

> She would sit Indian style on top of her desk and chain smoke cigarettes as she told the story of Mexico from memory.

I have incorporated some of her teaching style while homeschooling my own kids, minus the cigarettes of course.

When I went to Instituto Cervantes I became friends with a girl named Celia who lived near me. We decided to carpool to school together. Her mom was a wild driver. I was often car sick, but spending time with my friend and her mom gave me even more opportunities to absorb the language and culture.

Many days when I got home from school my mind was completely scrambled from information overload. I found it very difficult to speak English right when I got into the house. I usually would go to my room to have a bit of quiet time, or I would sit in the kitchen and talk in Spanish with our Mexican housekeeper, Odila.

In Mexico a girl's fifteenth birthday is as big of an event as her wedding. Traditionally the Quinceanera is a girl's coming out party.

I turned fifteen when we lived in San Luis Potosi. While I did not have a traditional Mexican party, I had one of my favorite birthdays ever.

I had a wonderful youth pastor named David Cerar and a wonderful group of friends from church. I loved every minute of my time with them.

My Youth Group in San Luis Potosi, Mexico

My church friends all came to my birthday party. We played crazy games and ate a giant birthday chocolate chip cookie. To wrap it all up my friend

Kristie chased me down and gave me fifteen birthday swats with a frying pan!

I had very mixed emotions when our year in San Luis came to a close. I was very sad to leave my friends and a city that I had fallen in love with, but I also was excited to see what was going to happen next. By this point in my life adventure and change was my norm. Staying still was not something I was used to.

Farewell Serenade

Just before we moved back to the states my friends stopped by with their guitars to serenade us. It was beautiful, just like you would expect from the movies. The singing and guitar playing may not have been expert enough for Hollywood, but to me it was perfect.

I am very thankful to have been able to visit my friends in San Luis many times over the years. They are still dear to my heart today.

Where God sent our family next was something we would have never imagined.

Strategy to Unlock Your Destiny

Adventure is Calling Your Name

I believe that everyone should go on a mission trip to another country at some point in their life. Getting outside of your own country and culture is a sure way to open a whole new view of God and the world to you.

God will have an inheritance of children from every nation on the earth. His heart is for every people group, so we might as well lean our hearts in that direction too.

One of the more recent countries I have traveled to is Cuba. I have enjoyed my time there so much. The first time I went, I felt such joy the moment I stepped off the plane and into the immigrations area of the airport.

It is like there is something in the atmosphere in Cuba that my spirit connects with.

As I spent time there walking along the ocean and riding the bus throughout the island, my spirit came alive more and more. The only way I can explain it is to say that the airways feel different there.

Each time I have gone, I have returned home with fresh clarity and vision for my life and my family. It is amazing what getting away to a different location can do for your focus.

There is something about physically going to another location that opens you up to a new level of connection with God.

One of the very best parts of my most recent trip was that I was able to take a few people with me. I absolutely loved seeing my team members come alive as God stirred up old and new things in their hearts.

One of the greatest joys of my life is to see people prosper in their souls. I love to see them living life to the fullest.

If you have ever considered going on a mission trip, please do it!

If you have never travelled outside of your home country, start by applying for your passport.

Destiny key: Life is too short to sit back and wait for something interesting to happen. We have to happen to life!

Don't let lack of finances stop you from going to the nations. When God puts the desire to go on a trip in your heart, He will provide all that you need to answer His call.

There is a saying in Argentina that when a baby is born it comes with a loaf of bread under its arm. God always sends provision with whatever He sends your way.

Here are some links for ministries that you can join up with in your adventure.

Leannegoffministries.org
Heartlandbttn.com
Globalawakening.com

Chapter 5

A Very Important Divine Appointment

God moved our family all the way from the mountains smack in the middle of Mexico, to the flat cornfields of Colfax, Iowa smack in the middle of the United States.

Colfax is a tiny town with about 2,000 people. We first went to Colfax to visit some ministry friends named Roger and Shirley Helle who were the executive directors of the Teen Challenge center there.

While we were spending time with their family, Roger hired my parents to work at Teen Challenge as the Evangelism and Outreach Directors. There we were, going about our own business, when God opened up this new door for our family.

My parents have always been completely up for anything God has led them to do. It is amazing what can happen when you are just minding your own business and living your life completely surrendered to the Lord.

As part of their job mom and dad would take the Teen Challenge students out to share the stories of how God had changed their lives and delivered them from all kinds of life controlling addictions.

They took the students to talk with people waiting in line outside of rock concerts, as well as people who were participating in Iowa's annual RAGBRAI bike ride. They took them to share their testimonies in many churches, prisons, and schools. They even took them to share with people at Mardi Gras in New Orleans.

> It is amazing what can happen when you are just minding your own business and living your life completely surrendered to the Lord.

About three times a year they would load up three vanloads of staff and students and drive three days to San Luis Potosi, Mexico. We would teach the students complicated dramas, dress them in elaborate costumes and mime makeup, and go out to the streets to perform. Crowds of people gathered very quickly to check out what we were doing.

After the drama performances someone would preach a short message and invite people to give their lives to Christ. Many people were saved through those outreaches.

Some people say that short-term mission trips are not effective, but I recently heard a story about a young girl from Russia named Anya. One day she went out to buy some eggs. As she was on her way to the store she stopped to listen to some foreign missionaries who were sharing the gospel in the street. She gave her heart to Jesus that day. Today she is married to a pastor's son and is in ministry.

Anya's story touched me deeply. So many times we did dramas and shared the gospel to crowds of women and children in the streets. Many of them would raise their hands to say that they wanted to give their hearts to Jesus, but we never really knew what happened to them afterwards.

There was a thought in some of our minds that if we were really successful, grown men would be coming to pray with us. It was almost like children were not as big of a catch. Now I know that children are key. The majority of people who are Christians make the decision to follow Christ when they are very young.

People all over the world are longing for the empty place in their heart to be filled. Most do not know that it is Jesus who they desire.

He told them, the harvest is plentiful, but the workers are few. Ask the Lord of the harvest, therefore, to send out workers into his harvest field. (Luke 10:2 NASB)

Jesus truly is the Desire of the Nations.

When we arrived in Iowa I was a year behind in high school. I probably learned a lot more the year I went to school in Mexico than at any other time in my school career, but I did not earn any credits for that year.

I set right to work on high school by correspondence. I worked hard to complete ninth and tenth grade in one year, and eleventh and twelfth grades the next year. This allowed me to graduate a whole year early. It is amazing what you can do when you set your mind to it!

Many days I got up at five in the morning to go to my job where I set tables and washed dishes at a nursing home. At 1:30 I would head home, take a much needed shower, and get to work on school for a few hours.

Some days when I worked in the nursing home kitchen I had to be to work at 7am, but I always preferred the days when I had to be there at 5:30am. It seems illogical, but somehow I always found that waking up much earlier was just easier. It is kind of like jumping right into a cold swimming pool instead of slowly edging your way in.

Our time at Teen Challenge was wonderful for many reasons. I loved the community aspects of our life there. All of the staff and students lived on the same property and shared meals together.

I was used to living with a lot of people close by. For years we either had people outside of our immediate family living with us, or we had lived with other people in their homes. One time we even had a guy who my parents found in the woods stay with us for a few days until we found him another place to live.

The Teen Challenge property in Colfax, Iowa is a very beautiful place. It sits on eighty acres and has great hills for sledding in the wintertime. Having been raised in the south I had never in my life experienced more than a very rare light dusting of snow.

We moved to Iowa in August, and that November we got eight inches of snow. I was delighted! It was absolutely beautiful. My friends and I spent hours sledding down the perfect hills on huge inner tubes until we couldn't stand the cold one moment longer.

One time we all piled onto the inner tube together. It was all fun and games until we ended up in a heap at the bottom of the hill. That hurt. My head ached, and I felt frozen through. My friends had to help me get home where my mom helped me into a warm bath.

There was a pond at the bottom of one of the hills. Once the pond froze over, the Teen Challenge guys would build a ramp out of the snow then sled down the hill, fly off the ramp, and over the frozen pond.

Jeffrey loved that ride. When I ask him today what he remembers about it, he enthusiastically says it was so much fun! If he ever got hurt doing it he does not remember it because the fun of it was so overwhelming.

Jeffrey has always put having fun as one of his highest priorities. I think the rest of our family could have learned something from him in that. I was always the more serious type, and I was definitely way too chicken to try that stunt!

> Jeffrey has always put having fun as one of his highest priorities. I think the rest of our family could have learned something from him in that.

One of my favorite times of the year at Teen Challenge was Christmas. I loved helping wrap all of the donated gifts for the students. It was so much fun to see the huge pile under the big tree in the lobby of the building. I also loved the feeling of joy and family as we all ate our Christmas feast together in the large dining room.

The very best and most important part of our move to Iowa was that within days of moving there I met the man that would one day become my husband. That was a divine set up!

Strategy to Unlock Your Destiny

Friendship: Who needs it?

There once lived two men called Damon and Pythias. They were both lovers of truth and integrity. In all the city of Syracuse they could find no one who upheld these principles as well as each other.

Dionysius was at that time the ruler of Syracuse. He wielded complete authority and very often abused his power, for he was very hot-tempered. If anyone angered him, they would be put to death.

One day Dionysius was informed that a young man named Pythias had been heard complaining against his cruelty. No one was allowed to criticise the ruler, and Dionysius condemned the youth to die.

When Pythias learned of his fate, he begged to be allowed to return home to set his affairs in order.

"How far away is your home?" enquired Dionysius suspiciously, "and how may I be certain you will return?"

"My home is many miles distant," replied

Pythias, "but I have a friend, Damon, who is willing to take my place while I am away."

There was a stir amongst the bystanders, and a man stepped to Pythias's side.

"*I* am Damon, my lord," he said. "I will give myself up as a pledge of my friend's return, and if any accident befalls him I will die in his stead."

The tyrant was amazed by this generosity, and gave Pythias permission to depart. He set a day and hour for the return, and warned that he would not fail to exercise justice on his friend if Pythias did not return in time.

The days passed and the morning dawned on which Pythias was to have been executed. Pythias did not appear. The people of Syracuse said that Damon would surely be killed.

Everyone agreed that Damon's behaviour was rash and foolish, but Damon himself was the happiest man in the prison. He was filled with hope that his friend would *not* return in time.

At the set moment, he was led out to execution with a cheerful face.

Dionysius had come to see him meet his

death, and called out to him in mocking words. "So, Damon, where is your friend, of whom you were so confident? I fear you have allowed him to take advantage of your simplicity."

"It is impossible for me to doubt my friend's loyalty" replied Damon. "Perhaps he has met with some accident along the way."

At that moment a horse broke through the crowd. Pythias, travel-stained and weary, half fell out of his saddle and ran to embrace his friend.

"I have come – in time," he gasped. "My horse was killed, and I could not find another. Thank heaven I am in time to save you!"

But Damon did not want Pythias to die. He pleaded with Pythias to allow his execution to continue. The tyrant Dionysius watched in disbelief as each friend eagerly sought to give up his life for the other.

"Cease, cease these debates," he exclaimed, stepping forward and taking their hands. "I hereby set both of you free. Never in my life have I seen such loyalty, nor did I dream such a thing could exist. I beg you will accept my pardon and allow me to share in your friendship."

Damon and Pythias – first told around the 4th century B.C.

4th century B.C.

Greater love has no one than this, that one lay down his life for his friends. (John 15:13)

Friendship is about the desire to be known. We were created for connection. The reason God made us in the first place was so that He could have relationship with us. He hardwired this same desire for relationship into our makeup.

Here are seven tips to help you foster community and practice hospitality:

- **Practice** smiling at people and looking them in the eye.

- **Practice** making small talk. This doesn't come naturally to everyone, but it is the starting point for deeper conversations.

- **Don't wait** until your house is perfect to invite people over for dinner. If your house is messy your guests will just feel better about their own home. You will be doing them a service.

- **Don't wait** for someone to invite you for coffee. Take the first step.

- Make a phone call or text **instead of waiting** for someone to call you.

- When people make room for you in their lives, take it, even if it's just hanging out with them and helping them with whatever project they are working on. That may be all the time they have available, so **honor it.**

- In order to make meaningful connections you must **be intentional.** Get out your calendar and make a plan.

YOU are the solution to lack of community!

Strangers are just friends waiting to happen. ~Rod McKuen

A man who has friends must himself be friendly. (Proverbs 18:24a)

Destiny key: Ask the Lord to bring the people that you need into your life. Ask Him to naturally remove the ones that are holding you back from your destiny and to help them find their place to thrive elsewhere.

Chapter 6

Dating Woes

We have probably all heard someone say, "The first moment I saw my future spouse I knew they were the one for me." That is definitely not the way it happened to me.

I clearly remember the first moment I saw Christopher. He walked into the back door of the Teen Challenge building, and I literally thought "Wow, who is that!"

> The first time I saw him
> I thought, "Wow, who is that!"

He was twenty-one years old, had long hair, and was overall mysterious. I was only fifteen. I definitely did not think I would ever be an option in his mind. I had no idea that one day, far in the future, romance would come to us.

Soon after I first saw Christopher I learned that he had just finished a two-month outreach with YWAM in the Amazon jungle. That was an instant connection point for our families. He had plenty of interesting stories and pictures to share about life on a boat in the Amazon River.

During his time in Brazil he could not help but pick up a few words of Portuguese. When he discovered that I spoke Spanish, he was determined to compare the languages. I guess he eventually decided that Portuguese would be very difficult to learn in Colfax, Iowa, but that Spanish might be possible.

He started asking me how to say all kinds of different things in Spanish. He would ask me to teach him, but I did not take his request very seriously. I was used to people asking me to teach them Spanish, but they were never really willing to put any effort into learning a language. It was like they thought I could somehow transfer Spanish to them without them having to work at it.

Because of my fatigue with this "teach me Spanish" request, I handed Christopher a book, told him to complete an assignment I had marked out, and to get back to me after he had done it. I figured that would get me off the hook.

Every couple days he would come back to me and ask me to teach him something in Spanish. I would reply, "Did you do the homework I gave you? Come to me after you finish it."

Finally, he got the message and did the homework. From there we embarked on a friendship that almost was entirely lived out in Spanish.

Christopher has a wonderful quality about him where he dives into whatever he sets his mind to do 110%. He listened to music and sermons in Spanish. He attended Spanish churches and talked to any Spanish speaking person he could find. He went out to the areas of Des Moines where a lot of Hispanics live and talked to them on the streets and in restaurants.

> At the time, neither of us could have told you why he was so consumed with a desire to learn Spanish. We had no idea that God was preparing him to minister in Latin America.

At the time, neither of us could have told you why he was so consumed with a desire to learn Spanish. We had no idea that God was preparing him to minister in Latin America. Today he is very comfortable preaching in Spanish and has started preaching in Portuguese as well.

If you were to ask him what is the best way to learn another language, he would tell you that in order to speak good Spanish you have to speak bad Spanish first. You have to be willing to try and to fail. Fear of looking like a fool is pride.

God resists the proud, but gives grace to the humble (James 4:6). If you are willing to humble yourself and work at it, you can learn.

Six years went by while Christopher and I grew to be best friends. Feelings of attraction come and go when you pass through that many years, but an undeniable deep care and love developed between the two of us. We considered ourselves as brother and sister. Our families did not see it like that at all. They saw that we were meant for each other before we did. But I will tell you more about that later.

After two years living in Iowa, my parents transferred to Teen Challenge in Omaha, Nebraska. I went through a very hard time during that season. Christopher had started up a relationship with one of my best friends, and I was sincerely happy for them.

Around the same time, I became romantically involved with a guy who had gone through the Teen

Challenge program. Things seemed good at first, but after a while they started to turn sour.

I am a very loyal person, and I found it very hard to call the relationship quits. On top of my natural tendency to be very loyal, I had received some teaching about courtship that confused my thinking. The message that I absorbed from this teaching was that casual dating was not godly. It was almost like you either had to not be attracted to a person at all, or you had to be completely in for the long haul. I did not feel the liberty to casually date a person in order to find out if they had good character or if we had anything in common.

The person I was in a relationship with had a lot of unresolved childhood issues in his life. The closer we became, the more those issues affected me. After a while we got engaged, and the struggles multiplied. I did not realize it for some time, but I eventually found out that he had taken up his old life style and was shooting up drugs.

He was absolutely miserable. A load of guilt was pressing down hard on him. He would sometimes talk about how he was thinking about killing himself. One time when we were driving down the road he started to drive really fast and said he was looking for a brick wall to drive into. I felt torn up inside and trapped. I thought that if I broke up with him, he might actually kill himself, and it would be on my head.

I was so stressed out that I lost a lot of weight. My personality was not what it had been, and I felt completely lost.

Calling off a wedding is a very hard thing to do. I believe that many people get married even though they are not sure that they should, simply because it is embarrassing to admit that you have gotten in so deep against your better judgment.

> I felt torn up inside and trapped. I thought that if I broke up with him, he might actually kill himself, and it would be on my head.

One day around the time I became engaged, a dear lady named Sandra Collier, who is a mother in the faith, said something very disturbing to me. She said, "Even if you get to the moment where you are about to walk down the aisle and want to change your mind, it will not be too late." I never forgot her words. They haunted me. I am so thankful that Sandra was sensitive to Holy Spirit and was not afraid to speak up and be a mother.

Six weeks before the wedding, just as we were getting ready to drop the invitations into the mail, my dad did what I did not have the strength to do. He postponed the wedding. Now, I was a legal adult and could have gotten married anyway, but I had a deep love and loyalty to my dad that won out over everything else. My dad is my hero! He saved the day!

Whew! What a relief! My dad's courageous step gave me the strength to make a clean break and move forward with my life.

> God had a call on my life, and the enemy did his best to try to prevent me from living out my destiny.

While I was on my lunch break at work I called the guy and told him I was done. When I got home from work there was a pile of stuff by my front door. He had dropped off everything he had that reminded him of me. It was over!

Some people may have wondered at the immediate change in me. Maybe they wondered how I could get over a broken engagement so seemingly easy. I did sympathize with the guy and hoped that he would be able to move on with his life and get the help he needed. I had been living in such torment for so long that the strongest feeling I had when our relationship ended was relief.

God had a call on my life, and the enemy did his best to try to prevent me from living out my destiny. The enemy tried to distract me, but he always pushes things too far. He overplayed his hand, and he lost.

I am so thankful to my earthly father Ray Goff and to my heavenly Father for loving me and rescuing me at my darkest moment. Hallelujah!

After all that I went through, I was able to make a fresh start and move forward with my life. I started attending Bellevue Christian Center in Bellevue, Nebraska and met some wonderful life-long friends.

God used a woman named Julaine Christensen to breathe life back into my soul. She loved on me and pulled me into teaching worship dance to girls at the church. My whole life I had loved ballet. I had taken ballet classes in Mexico and in Iowa, and Julaine pulled on that area of my life to activate me into ministry. That was a lifeline for me. Julaine is a real mother to so many.

After a time of healing and rest I felt that it was time for me to step back into YWAM. This decision launched me back into international travel and so many wonderful adventures.

Shortly before I took off for YWAM the enemy took another stab at taking me out. My mom and I were in Iowa visiting friends in the wintertime. We were getting ready to head back to Nebraska, and we decided to drive to Des Moines to do some shopping on our way home.

Christopher decided he would join us for the shopping trip and say goodbye at the mall. My mom drove her car, and Christopher and I followed behind in his. Right before we got into his car, he spontaneously asked me if I wanted to drive. I chose poorly and agreed.

> We were flying down the interstate when I realized I had lost control of the car. I very calmly said, "Christopher, help."

A couple of days prior to this, a big snowstorm had come through the area and made a big mess, but most of it had cleared up by the time we headed out to the mall. It was a beautiful, sunny day. As we were driving Christopher causally said, "Watch out for that patch of ice ahead." As soon as he said it, he realized it was a mistake to point it out to me. My natural instinct was to tap the brakes.

We were flying down the interstate when I realized I had lost control of the car. I very calmly said, "Christopher, help." That is the last thing I remember until I woke up as paramedics were preparing to put me into an ambulance.

What I later found out was that as we slid to the right side of the interstate we narrowly missed hitting an eighteen-wheeler. I don't remember it at all, but to this day I have to fight to keep my peace when I'm near an eighteen-wheeler on the interstate.

Less than an hour before we went off the road, another car went off in the same exact spot. The driver had left to get help. While he was gone the car I was driving slammed into his. The accident would not have been quite so bad if the other car had not been there. The driver of the other car must have been so shocked when he came back.

When we crashed I hit my head on the thin strip of car body that is between the windshield and the driver's window. I had a concussion and was knocked out. My hair was full of broken glass; my lap was full of snow.

Christopher was very worried about me. He said that when I opened my eyes they looked so weird. I didn't speak at first. He tried speaking to me in English and Spanish just in case I had forgotten one of my languages. He was very relieved when I finally spoke. I honestly cannot remember which language came out of my mouth.

From the rear view mirror of her car, my mom saw the whole accident take place. She got to us as fast as she could. I could hear her screaming to see if we were okay.

A lot of other drivers also stopped to see if there was anything they could do to help. People were so kind. Everything was surreal for me as they put me into the ambulance and drove me to the hospital. They ran a lot of tests and kept me for a couple of days.

After I got home it took a long time for all of the soreness to wear off. I had headaches every day for a year and many nights slept on the floor because the bed felt too soft for my shaken up body. I still deal with tension in my neck and headaches at times. It took my parents weeks to get me behind the steering wheel of a car again.

Christopher didn't get hurt in the accident, but he did lose his glasses, his guitar (which got smashed in the trunk), and his car. It was an older car, but he had just paid it off and switched the insurance from comprehensive to liability.

> Years later he told me that he
> had come very close to kissing me
> on the forehead and telling
> me that he loved me as I laid
> in the hospital bed.

Thankfully Christopher forgave me for wrecking his car. His dad asked him later if the accident had drawn the two of us closer together. Christopher told him that he thought it had. He experienced a lot of emotions as he was helping to take care of me in the hospital. Years later he told me that he had come very close to kissing me on the forehead and telling me that he loved me as I laid in the hospital bed.

I believe that the enemy wanted to take us both out. In the long run he lost out because God hooked Christopher and I up into a powerful team.

Strategy to Unlock Your Destiny

Can a Godly Person Have Boundaries?

Boundaries indicate limits. They are the fence around you that keeps good things in and bad things out.

I have a chain link fence in my back yard. We paid good money to have it built, because we had small kids who we wanted to keep safe. We also wanted to keep the neighbor's large dogs from walking right up to our back door and trying to come inside our house.

Boundaries are not:

1. An excuse to be selfish or rude.

2. A way to turn you into me.

3. A way to control other people.

Making demands is a form of control. You cannot demand of someone and show honor to them at the same time.

Do nothing out of selfish ambition or vain conceit. Rather, in humility value others above yourselves, not looking to your own interests but each of you to the interests of the others. (Phil. 2:3-4)

Healthy boundaries are:

1. A way to be healthy in order to love God and others well.

2. A way to protect other people from you.

3. A tool to give you power to control yourself.

You do not get to control other people. You are the only person you can control.

You are only responsible for the things in your own yard. The kinds of things that are in your yard are YOUR:

- Feelings

- Attitudes

- Beliefs

- Behaviors

- Actions

- Choices

- Thoughts

- Values

- Limits

- Talents

- Strengths

- Desires

- Passions

- Love

You are NOT responsible for these in other people. You only get to control YOU.

It is not your job to keep everyone around you happy. You cannot afford to work harder on other people's lives than they are willing to.

Boundaries are all about self-control. They are about having a plan so that you can be who you need to be, to accomplish the call God has on your life.

An example of a good boundary with time is:

Don't let other people push you to make a quick decision. Take the time you need to think things through. Tell the person you will get back to them. Then be sure to show them honor by following through.

An example of a boundary with your words is: boundaries in your speech.

Do everything without complaining or arguing, so that you may become blameless and pure, children of God without fault in a crooked and depraved generation, in which you shine like stars in the universe. (Phil 2: 14-15)

You get to choose what comes out of your own mouth. You do not get to pick what other people say. Let your words create life.

An example of boundaries with your attitude is:

If you're grumpy, send yourself to your room, go for a drive, or take a walk. You need to protect other people from you. This is a great way to preserve a peaceful atmosphere in your family. You can just tell your family that you need a time out.

Here is a clear boundary for your thought life:

Finally, brothers and sisters, whatever is true, whatever is noble, whatever is right, whatever is pure, whatever is lovely, whatever is admirable—if anything is excellent or praiseworthy—think about such things. (Phil. 4:8)

What can you do when someone hurts you? Matthew 18 lays out the solution very clearly.

1. *If your brother sins, go and point out their fault, just between the two of you. If they listen to you, you have won them over.*

2. *But if they will not listen, take one or two others along, so that every matter may be established by the testimony of two or three witnesses.*

3. *If they still refuse to listen, tell it to the church; and if they refuse to listen even to the church, treat them as you would a pagan or a tax collector.*

When you go to talk to the person who has offended you, your motive needs to be to restore unity, not to pick at the other person or try to make them be just like you.

Always assume the best about the other person. Say something like, "I am probably missing something, but I feel like (insert the feeling and specific incident). Can you help me understand the situation better?"

If you do not feel that the situation is resolved, pull in an impartial, mature mediator to help you.

If you still cannot get to a place of unity, you will want to bring the matter to your pastor or leader.

Can a godly person have boundaries? Did Jesus have boundaries?

1. Jesus often went away alone to pray even though the crowds were pressing in for His attention.

2. He did not get off track with other people's agendas for His life. He said that He only did what His Father was doing and saying.

3. He said that He is the ONLY way to the Father. No one can get to the Father except through Him.

Destiny key: Ask Jesus to show you any boundaries you need to make or any walls you need to tear down.

Chapter 7

My Very Own Adventure

Have you ever been seasick? I mean, so very seasick that you daydream about jumping overboard just to make it stop!

I was nineteen years old when I joined YWAM's Mercy Ships South Pacific. Mercy Ships are floating hospitals that sail to third world nations to provide medical relief.

I bought my plane ticket to Australia, and set out to the other side of the world on my own.

A friend from my church named Brian and I decided to go to the DTS school onboard Mercy Ships together. Having a friend to go with was so helpful. Brian bought his ticket and took off two weeks before me to visit family in Sydney. I bought my plane ticket to Newcastle, Australia, and set out to the other side of the world on my own. I clearly remember the first moments of my flight. I was a bundle of excitement and nervousness. I had gotten a little used to flying by this point in my life, but the whole thing was still a little unnerving.

When I was young there was a little girl who went to our church in New Orleans who was killed when an airplane crashed into her home just after take-off. She basically burned to death. The girl and I were about the same age. Hearing the story about her tragic death made me not only very aware of my own mortality, it plain scared me.

> The enemy studies us and does His best to stop us from living our lives for God's kingdom.

The first time I flew I was in fourth grade. My brother and I flew together from Houston to New Orleans to visit our grandparents. I shivered and cried almost the whole flight. I honestly believe that the enemy used the story of the little girl from our church to put fear into me as part of his strategy to hold me back from the call on my life.

The enemy studies us and does his best to stop us from living our lives for God's kingdom. He is always working to scare, distract, accuse, and condemn us.

As I got older I took on the attitude that when it is my time to die, it will be my time to die. When I fly I might as well sit back and relax since I have no control over the airplane anyway. Every time I got onto a plane I would tell that to myself and put my life into God's hands again.

The ship that we lived on was called Island Mercy. She was a lovely home full of wonderful people from all over the world. We spent three months docked in Newcastle while we took Bible classes on subjects like: the Father heart of God, Intercession, Worship, Inductive Bible Study, and Christ in You. Each week a different teacher would come to teach a new subject.

One week a group of surfers from another YWAM base in town joined us for classes. That was really interesting for someone like me who grew up mostly landlocked.

During the lecture phase of our school we also sorted through a warehouse full of donated eyeglasses and medical supplies that we were going to take to the islands on our outreach. We had work duties in the afternoons which included things like preparing meals, washing dishes, cleaning bathrooms, chipping paint, and painting the ship.

After the lecture part of our school was completed it was time to set sail. The excitement of preparing to go to sea was contagious. Everyone was in preparation mode. We all did last minute shopping and cleaned our cabins.

The Island Mercy

The experienced sailors told us to tie everything down in our cabins. I tied stuff down, but I had no clue how important that task would turn out to be. I really do not know what I thought sailing would be like, but I promise you I had no idea it was going to be as rough as it turned out to be.

I had no clue that I would be susceptible to seasickness. I was just excited to set out to sea. I had some milk and chocolate mint cookies taking up space in the community refrigerator. A few hours before we set sail I decided to finish them off as part of our clean out the fridge chore.

I desperately regretted that decision as soon as we got out of the harbor. I spent my first night at sea hugging the toilet. I can still clearly see the floor of the particular bathroom I was in. It was so awful.

Eventually I emptied my stomach sufficiently and made my way to my bunk. The ship was rolling so much that I bounced from one side of the hallway to the other with each sway of the ship.

> I really do not know what I thought sailing would be like, but I promise you I had no idea it was going to be as rough as it turned out to be.

Spin around in circles for a few minutes, then swing on a swing set, then ride on a merry-go-round and you might feel what I was feeling. But to take it a step further, you can't get off! You cannot just say, "Ok guys, I am not doing too well, can we just be done now?" The realization that I was going to be living like that for the foreseeable future was intense.

I yearned for the faith to command the waves and wind to be still. In my mind's eye I can still see the churning ocean as I look over the railing on the ship's deck. Blah.

I remember my friends telling me to get up on deck and look out to the horizon. Wow! It was amazing what a difference that made!

When I would look straight down into the sea, I would feel like I was going to die, but when I would take deep breaths and look at the spot where the sky meets the sea, I could rest much easier.

After a couple days I was very relieved to get my sea legs. I actually started feeling good enough to get out of bed and be a productive team member. Even though I was feeling a bit better, adjusting to living in constant motion was still very interesting.

There were five of us girls living in my cabin. I slept in a top bunk that had five small cupboards under it that served as our closets. Connected to the foot of my bed was another top bunk, which meant that another girl's head was just below my feet. One night as we were all sleeping the ship was rolling so much that I actually slid right out of my bunk and into the other girl's bed!

Things could get really crazy in the dining room. Between meal times the chairs would slide back and forth from one side of the room to the other. There were many times where I had to sit at the table and wrap my legs around the table leg to keep from sliding away. Then I had to wrap my left arm around my plate and hold my cup with my left hand while I ate with my right hand.

When the sea was calm we could get away with just setting the dishes on little rubber mats, but when the wind picked up things would get really wild.

Imagine trying to take a shower under those conditions. You can't just stand under the water and wash your hair; you have to kind of chase the water while trying to keep your balance. When you are at sea, fresh water conservation is very important which meant we were only allowed one minute of having the shower water turned on each day. Things got pretty smelly when the air conditioner stopped working.

> Imagine trying to take a shower under these conditions. You can't just stand under the water and wash your hair; you have to kind of chase the water while trying to keep your balance.

I worked in the galley (kitchen) for most of my time on the ship. Imagine what it would be like to cook at sea. We had to use bungee cords to strap everything down. One time the bungee cord that held the silverware container in place came undone. The silverware flew into the dining room and started sliding from one side of the room to the other. That was the only time in my life I have ever chased silverware. Talk about the fork running away with the spoon!

We sailed from Newcastle, Australia to Papua New Guinea for our outreach trip. When we arrived at the dock we were greeted by natives dressed in their traditional island way. They did traditional dances to the beat of drums to honor us.

We dropped off teams of people in two different cities. These teams lived on the island with the

> Some of the tribes they stayed with were cannibalistic just one generation back.

natives for several weeks. They slept in huts or outside and used mosquito nets at night. Some of the tribes they stayed with were cannibalistic just one generation back.

I was very happy that I got approved to be on the optical team, which stayed with the ship. We went on to another city where we set up optical clinics during the day and went home to the ship at night.

The clinics we ran had several stations. First we had the patient read a standard eye test chart, and we wrote down their results on a small piece of paper. Next they had to stop at the refraction test machine where we added more information to their "chart." After that, our team optometrist would test them to determine their prescription.

Once we had their correct prescription we would sort through piles of donated glasses until we found a pair that was as close as possible to what they needed.

There was no room for fashion in this process. To these people being able to see well was worth wearing whatever type of frame was available. Finally, we would heat the frames and adjust them to fit the best they could.

We spent many long, hot days serving long lines of people. I was so glad to be able to go back to the ship to rest at night. The people on the teams that we had dropped off in other cities did not have that luxury.

At that time Papua New Guinea was experiencing a lot of unrest. The atmosphere felt very oppressive. The government had declared a nine o'clock curfew each night. If a person was caught out after nine, they would be put in jail.

Traveling on a ship is convenient in that you get to take your whole house with you wherever you go. People joke about packing so much that they even pack their kitchen sink, but when you travel on a ship you literally do take your kitchen sink with you. That was one part about sailing that I really appreciated.

After our outreach was finished we picked up the other teams and sailed back to Australia. Our school was done, and it was time to say goodbye and go home to our own countries. I knew in my heart that my time with the Island Mercy was not over. I would definitely be going back.

I also had a sense that I would end up married to Christopher, but I had no idea how it would come about.

Strategy to Unlock Your Destiny

Your Natural Default

The city that I live in seems to be in a competition with Chicago for the title of "Windy City." We regularly get high winds blowing in over the flat prairie. The wind has made our home life very interesting.

1. When we have a combination of snow and wind, we almost always end up with a 2 or 3 foot snow drift covering our driveway. The crazy thing is that the yard will be nearly snow free. For some reason the way our house is situated causes the wind to pick the snow up from the yard and drop it into the drive way.

2. We have had two trampolines over the years. The first one blew away in the middle of the night. The wind picked it up and carried it all the way down the street, past 5 or 6 houses, and dropped it into a pond where it presumably still is today. As the trampoline traveled down the street, it left pieces of itself along the way in the neighbors' yards. We had to pay $160 to repair our neighbor's fence. We tied the second trampoline down firmly, but it eventually wore out from use, so we got rid of it.

3. A few years ago my parents gave the kids a basketball goal for Christmas. It was the kind that you put sand in to weigh it down, as opposed to the kind that you cement into the ground. Even with 300 pounds of sand, the wind regularly blew it over. We had to be careful to not park the car near it on windy days. Eventually one of the metal rods that held the goal up, snapped clean through because of the pressure from the wind.

When my husband and I woke up one windy morning, we both had the same thought. We experienced a moment of worry, only to breathe a sigh of relief when we remembered that we had nothing left in the yard to blow away.

We laughed together, and Christopher said, "That was like phantom worry." It was kind of like the stories you hear about amputees who still feel sensations from their missing limbs. Or maybe what more of us can relate to, the feeling of your phone vibrating when it really isn't.

It made me think, how many of the things we worry about are even reality? Maybe a huge portion of our worry is only a matter of habit. What do you think?

Did you know that you can live in perfect peace? Did you know that fear and worry are tools of the enemy to keep you from your destiny? I am so tired of the enemy tricking us into thinking that fear and worry are some kind of normal emotions.

It seems to be socially acceptable to worry about our kids or family members. That's nuts. Fear is an evil spirit that we can choose to stand against or to agree with.

We need to see the battle for what it is and fight. Let's not agree with the enemy and let him have a place to rule in our hearts.

Be aware of your self-talk....the voices in your head. Every single thought you have is not your own. The devil whispers lies constantly, and we have to practice recognizing them and not agreeing with them.

It is great to have a healthy friend or parent to tell your thoughts to. They should be able to help you decide where each thought is coming from.

When we agree with God's thoughts towards us, we grow in peace and joy. When we agree with the enemy, we open the door for him to come in and destroy our peace.

Holy Spirit is our Friend and Helper. We need Him so much. As we take time to value Him and soak in His presence, He fills us up with peace and joy.

The enemy will do everything he can to keep you from living in peace. Quieting the heart does not come natural to everyone. Living in peace is a skill that you can practice.

As children of God, it is our nature to love. It is **not** our nature to live in fear. Practice until peace and joy become your natural default.

I want to share with you an experience my spiritual daughter had with the Lord. I love it so much because it's all about abiding in peace and expanding the kingdom.

I had the craziest experience with the Lord. We were standing in a train station, and I could literally feel the air from the trains pushing against my face and back.

I was like, "Hey, I hate trains."

Jesus was like, "Let yourself go."

The wind totally held me up.

He said, "That's abiding in peace."

Then we walked onto the train, but it was still moving so fast. He was telling me the importance of abiding in peace and asked if I wanted to see something cool.

I said, "Yes."

We got off the train, and the station was crowded. Everyone was frozen, and Jesus said, "Watch this."

He went and began to change people's faces, their expressions.

He was like, "You try it."

We literally ran through the crowd taking casts off people and taking their crutches. We would just stretch out the person's legs or arms, and they were better.

Then we went back on the train. He told me that I can travel faster in peace than any other way.

~Ashley Reddish

Destiny key: It is very hard, if not impossible, to hear God's clear voice when you are not in peace.

Don't focus on all the chaos swirling around you. Take time to imagine Jesus sitting on His throne in heaven. He sits there in complete peace and rest. He is not worried one bit.

As you choose to lift your focus to the Lord, peace and clarity will flood your soul!

Chapter 8

Finding my Bearings

Two weeks before I joined Mercy Ships my parents moved to Chattanooga, Tennessee to launch a women's program at Teen Challenge of the Mid-South. This meant that I came "home" to a city and home that I barely knew.

To say I felt a bit out of orbit would be very true. I did not have any friends there, but not to worry; two of my friends from the Mercy Ship decided to come stay with us for a few months.

I had to pay off my plane ticket from my trip to Australia, and I was determined to save up enough money to go back to the ship for another eight months. My friends Faith and Jen were taking time to decide what they were going to do next in life.

The three of us got jobs waiting tables at the same restaurant. We worked long and hard to reach our goals.

While Faith and Jen were with us, my mom decided to take us girls for a weekend trip to Pensacola, Florida. She took us to a church there named Brownsville Assembly that was having a world famous revival. The place was packed with people from all over the world. We had to stand in line to get into the service and then sit in an overflow auditorium.

The presence of God in the place was very strong. During worship I found myself telling God what kind of man I wanted to marry. Right away I clearly heard Him say, "You are [going to marry a man like that], and it is Christopher." It was so clear that I felt stunned but also like "duh." Our parents and friends all knew that Christopher and I were meant for each other, but it just was not completely obvious to either of us.

> During worship I found myself telling God what kind of man I wanted to marry.

After the service Mom took us girls out to eat. As we sat around the table we talked about what we had experienced at the revival service. I took the plunge and told them what God had spoken to me. They were all giddy girl excited. It was so embarrassing. I tried to calm them all down. After all, it did not matter much at all what I felt if Christopher was not on the same page!

They all wanted to know if I was going to tell Christopher about it. I told them that if he called before midnight that very night and specifically asked me what God spoke to me at the service, I would tell him.

> Every time the phone rang
> everyone was on high alert.

That was a funny night. Every time the phone rang everyone was on high alert. I was so nervous. I was beginning to think that I was off the hook when shortly before midnight the phone rang…..it was him!

I thought, "Okay, he still may not ask me what God spoke to me." That was a silly thought. Of course that question was the main reason he had called me in the first place.

We chatted for a while. Then he said, "So, did God speak anything to you at the services?"

Gulp, I said, "He told me who I am going to marry."

I thought maybe he would drop the conversation with that, but nope. Of course, he responded, "Who is it?"

I took a deep breath and said, "It's you." (Insert very long pause.)

Then I told him that I completely understood that he would have to know for himself. I said that I was planning to go back to Mercy Ships very soon and maybe God was just testing me to see if I would do what He said. I was honestly trying to let us both off the hook. It was painfully awkward.

Christopher said something like, "Yeah, maybe so," and we ended the call.

He did not call me back for three weeks! That was a very long time for us to go without talking.

When we eventually talked again, he said he had not heard anything clear from the Lord. I was fine with that. I did not understand how God could be telling me to go back to Mercy Ships and to marry Christopher anyway. I couldn't do them both at the same time.

After waiting tables for four months I managed to save up enough money to head back to the ship. I flew to Sydney, Australia and caught a train the rest of the way to Newcastle. I arrived just a day before we were to set sail.

We sailed up the east coast of Australia stopping in different cities to speak about Mercy Ships. My job on the ship's crew was working in the galley. I started off my time by washing dishes and cleaning floors. After a while I was asked to make salads and chop vegetables.

I spent many afternoons peeling and chopping huge piles of potatoes. Eventually I was taught to cook the main meat dishes. I went from not knowing much about cooking, to being able to plan and prepare whole meals for a hundred people.

Cooking on a ship is high risk. Sharp knives and boiling water take on a whole new danger level when the room is tilting back and forth. The stove had adjustable fence like railings that you put around the huge pots to keep them from sliding around. When it was time to drain a huge pot of boiling potatoes you had to time it just right so that the ship's movement would send you to the part of the kitchen you wanted to go to.

After our tour of the east coast of Australia we laid in a supply of groceries to last a couple of months. We were preparing to head to Vanuatu for an outreach. It is a nice feeling to see pantries and freezers stuffed full of food. Once we set out, we would have to stick to our menus and make the supplies last. We had to use the perishable food items in the first couple weeks, and use the non-perishable ones later on.

Eggs were especially tricky after we had been at sea for several weeks. It is next to impossible to know if an egg is rotten just by looking at it. We had to crack eggs into a bowl one at a time so we wouldn't risk contaminating several good eggs with a rotten one. If we cracked open a rotten one we would immediately run out the back door of the galley, up the stairs, out onto the deck, and throw it overboard as fast as we could.

Rotten eggs smell so bad, and there were no windows that could be opened in the galley while we were sailing. The ocean would have come rushing right in!

I loved working with the team in the galley. Sometimes when we would get cabin fever we would blast music and act completely crazy.

> There were no windows that could be opened in the galley while we were sailing. The ocean would have come rushing right in!

When we were in the islands the natives gave us fresh fruit all of the time. We had huge bunches of bananas hanging all over the galley. One time we held a "guess how many bananas" contest. There were literally hundreds of bananas.

We had so many bananas, coconuts, pineapple, papaya, and star fruit that it was impossible to eat it all. We had to toss the excess overboard before crossing country water lines. I guess the fish enjoyed it.

When you live in a country with British roots you must drink hot tea. Morning tea, mid-morning tea, dinner (lunch time) tea, afternoon tea, tea (evening meal) tea, and tea with supper (dessert) in the evening is standard. I take my tea with a bit of milk and sugar. All of this tea drinking brought people into the dining room at all hours.

I really enjoyed baking cookies for everyone. Crew members would stop by the galley at all hours of the day to see if there was anything special to eat. The galley and dining room were the heart of the ship. Being there fit my life's calling to motherhood.

Ever since I was a very little girl all I wanted to do was to get married and be a mother. I remember standing in Granny's kitchen when I was around seven years old when my Aunt Joanie said, "Beth, you are going to be a very good mom." I am sure she doesn't remember saying that to me, but those words went deep into my heart. She called forth and helped to awaken my destiny.

There is nothing like being out on the open sea. It is breathtaking. The sunrises and sunsets are indescribable. The dolphins swimming at the bow and the flying fish are simply amazing. The first time I heard about flying fish I thought it was a joke. I was so amazed to find out that they really exist.

Flying fish pop out of the water up to twenty feet in the air and glide at speeds around forty miles per hour for up to one hundred sixty feet before they dive back into the water. It is a mesmerizing thing to watch.

In Vanuatu the crew spent their time giving free dental and optical care to people who were lost in time. The engineering crew repaired the hospital's broken generator. They had been without electricity for a long time. They also repaired some really old sewing machines the natives had.

Many of the people we reached out to spent their whole lives living in grass huts. They lived off of the tropical fruit that grew all around them and the fish that they pulled from the sea.

> Many of the people we reached out to spent their whole lives living in grass huts.

Each time before we would set out to sea I would study the ocean to see how much foam was stirring, trying to assess how much the ship would pitch when we got underway. Thankfully, we seemed to have more calm days sailing than rough ones.

While we were in Vanuatu we spent a whole month anchored out a little way from the island where we were ministering. Twice a day teams of people would climb into small boats to motor over to the land.

This island was very remote. Think Gilligan's Island plus a couple hundred people. They did have a small airport. It was a flat piece of land which had a pole with a windsock stuck to it.

One time I went to move a large container of silverware and caught the cord of a large coffee pot by accident. Hot water spilled on my foot and burned it badly. I still have a scar from it. I needed to keep the wound dry, so if I made the trip to the island someone had to lift me from the lifeboat and carry me onto the beach.

After we were anchored off the island for a few weeks, the ship's saltwater converter stopped working. We had to head out of there a few days early because we were running out of drinking water.

When your drinking water is tainted with salt there is not really anything you can do to make it palatable. I tried mixing it with powdered milk and chocolate, and with a fruit flavored drink mix, but the saltiness still bled through. Saltwater can make you very sick too. So, we headed for an unplanned stop in New Caledonia.

We only stayed in New Caledonia for a couple of days. We just needed to take on fresh water and some other supplies. I really enjoyed my time there. It was very different, much more modern than the other islands that we visited.

The people on the other islands we spent time at spoke Pidgin English. The best way I can describe the language is that it sounded to me like a much more drastic form of the way Jar Jar Binks from Star Wars talks.

In New Caledonia they speak French. We were able to rest and take in the sights. I had the best tasting hamburger of my life in New Caledonia. It was almost completely raw and full of flavor. I do not know if it tasted so good because of the way it was prepared or because I had not eaten at a restaurant in such a long time.

After spending a few days sailing to New Zealand and a couple weeks with friends there, I boarded a plane and headed home to Tennessee just in time to spend Christmas with my family.

My friends really wanted me to spend a traditional Christmas at the beach with them in New Zealand, but I felt that it was time to go home. I left summertime in the islands and went to snowy winter in the Tennessee Mountains. It was a shock to my system.

I knew in my heart that my time with Mercy Ships was completed. I had to decide what to do next.

Strategy to Unlock Your Destiny

Discovering Your Special Sauce

What are you good at? Chances are you don't really know. Think about it for a second. Selah.

Ok, what did you come up with?

Most of the time the things we are truly good at don't even make the list. The things we are best at come to us so easily that we don't tend to even notice them. They can be a bit like water to a fish.

You might be able to identify the things you are best at by noticing what things you tend to judge the most in other people.

For example, if you always find yourself looking down on people who dress sloppy, you may have a gift for beauty. Maybe you could develop a practical solution to inspire others to dress for the life they want to have.

As natural human beings we tend to judge other people's weaknesses against our strengths. This is a primary recipe for disunity.

In reality, criticism is the opposite of honor. You cannot have a positive impact on society without honor.

Generally, it's a bad idea to compare yourself with other people. If you decide to compare other people's strengths to your own weaknesses, you could put yourself into a clinical depression.

We all have different strong points. No one has a monopoly on perfection.

As followers of Jesus, supernatural human beings, we get to come up higher and begin to value each other for the wide array of strengths that we each bring to the table.

It takes all kinds to get the work of the kingdom accomplished.

After all Jesus is the Head, and we are His body. I'm pretty sure He doesn't want to be all elbows.

Another way to find out what you should focus your life's efforts on is to think about what things in the world break your heart the most or make you feel intense anger.

In my case, thinking about orphans breaks my heart. There is something about the kids living in the slums in India that tears me up on the inside.

I know that part of my destiny is to rescue as many of them as I can. I want to see them not only provided for physically, but also nurtured emotionally and spiritually.

I cannot afford to get overwhelmed by the enormity of the problem. I have to take it one child at a time. For the past few years, our family has been sponsoring a little boy from India. My dream is to one day be able to provide for homes to care for multiple children there.

Another thing that makes me feel intense frustration is when I see angry parents being harsh with young children. Of course all parents experience moments of frustration, but spewing anger on kids is so damaging to their hearts. When I see a child wilt right before me, it breaks my heart.

My heart also breaks for the parents. Most of the time they never had nurturing parents themselves and are really orphans raising more emotional orphans.

It makes me want to swoop in and pour love and nurture on the parent and child alike.

The parents need someone to come alongside them and parent them. Only then will they have the life tools needed to stop the dysfunctional cycle they are living in.

The people who are the angriest about a

problem, are the ones who are to be the solution for it.

Destiny key: What makes you angry? What breaks your heart? Ask the Lord to show you what your part is in the solution.

Chapter 9

Marry Me

While I was on the other side of the world my dad did something very sneaky. He hired Christopher to work at Teen Challenge in Chattanooga. When I arrived home, Christopher was no longer living a dozen hours away in Iowa; he was living literally next door!

We were both very glad to see each other, but things were definitely awkward. We tried to act normal, but there were many moments when you could have cut the air with a knife.

> We tried to act normal, but there were many moments when you could have cut the air with a knife.

I was very ready to be married and to start a family. I knew that it was a huge part of my destiny, but it was something that I obviously could not accomplish on my own.

It was painful that every time I was interested in a guy, I seemed to be invisible to him, while the guys who paid attention to me were not realistic options in my mind.

I see now that God in His great love and wisdom was guarding over my life.

Christopher was very hesitant about marriage to anyone in general. A good friend who always taught single people only about the challenges of marriage, not the joys, had mentored him. This friend had a wonderful marriage, but really emphasized the importance of taking the decision to marry very seriously.

Christopher is a person who is very slow to make decisions in the first place. He is very careful and weighs choices from every possible angle many times over. While there was no doubt that he loved me deeply, the decision to marry anyone was overwhelming to him.

Things had really gotten to the place where we either had to stop being friends at all, or we had to move towards marriage.

What finally pushed him over the edge to take a step was the day when Sandra Collier casually mentioned to him that she felt like God was going to bring my husband into my life very soon, and that he was going to be tall.

Christopher is not quite 5'8". I guess Sandra's comment kind of scared him. He was not sure that he was ready to be married, but he was very sure that he did not want anyone else to marry me!

> He was not sure that he was ready to be married, but he was very sure that he did not want anyone else to marry me!

He decided that we should go out on one date as sort of a trial. He asked my dad's permission, which was happily granted.

I bought a new dress, we had our picture taken together, and he took me to Olive Garden. After six years of friendship it was all really weird yet completely natural at the same time.

He did not tell me at the time, but after that first date he knew that we were going to be married. He only needed time to save up money for an engagement ring. I did not know what he was thinking at all besides the fact that he asked me to go out again the next week.

Christopher may take a long time to make up his mind about something, but once he decides, he moves forward full force.

We went on our first date in May, got engaged in July, and married in October all of 1998. Every year he says that if he would have only known how great marriage would actually be, he would have proposed much sooner.

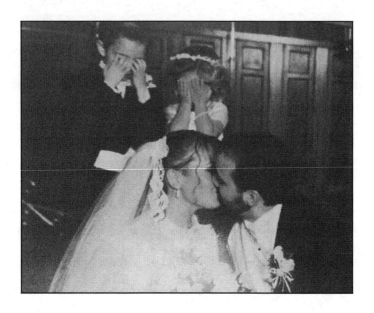

October 10, 1998

My whole life I had moved around so much that I was always saying tearful goodbyes to my friends. I had always looked forward to the day when I would be married to my best friend and never have to move away from them.

That day had finally come, and I have never regretted it. I knew that God had ordained for Christopher and I to join our lives together, but I did not realize at the time that Christopher also had a call on his life for the nations. It was not until years later that I learned about the time that God spoke to him about His dream to send Christopher around the world.

When Christopher was nineteen years old he went to his final year of summer church camp. He had gone to camp every year as a teenager, but had never experienced anything like what he experienced on the final night.

The minster preached a message calling people to surrender their lives into full-time ministry. Christopher cried through the whole sermon. At the end he went forward to the altar and wept intensely for a long time as he surrendered to God's call on his life.

When the service was over, and he had recovered, he started to do what all of the kids usually did and headed towards the snack bar to buy some candy and flirt with girls. On the way he heard God clearly tell him to come away and pray. He went out into the softball field and started to casually talk to God.

God clearly spoke to him, "I'm calling you to go to the nations to preach."

Christopher had no idea how it could happen. He was just a boy from a small Iowa town. In spite of how impossible it seemed to him, he was ready to obey.

Through everything that has happened in my life I can see a clear pattern of God's great wisdom and love for me. He had a dream for my life, He birthed His dream in my heart, and He is helping me to live it out.

When I get off track, He lovingly calls me back and works every step together for my good.

> When I get off track He lovingly calls me back and works every step together for my good.

You are a dream that God dreamed too. You have destiny inside of you. As you surrender every area of your heart to Him, He will be faithful to do His part.

Strategy to Unlock Your Destiny

Your Marriage Team

Do you ever struggle with figuring out what God's will is for your life? Sometimes we make discerning God's will more difficult than it has to be. In our sincere desire to carefully obey Him, we can overthink things and get really bogged down in decision making.

I have good news for you! It really doesn't have to be complicated.

Let's dial it back to the big picture. I would like to propose to you that discovering God's will all starts with GRATITUDE.

In everything give thanks, **for this is God's will for you** *in Christ Jesus.* (1 Thes. 5:18)

Our family takes time to sit at the table and eat dinner together most nights of the week. At every meal we go around the table and share one thing we are thankful for from that day.

Gratitude and grace go together. As you take time to give thanks to God (out loud is best), grace comes to you in every area of your life. This is a definite pathway to living in peace, and is the first step to finding out more specific details in regards to your destiny in God.

As Madam Blueberry says, "A THANKFUL HEART IS A HAPPY HEART."

How thankful are you?

Here are some questions to ask yourself about the person you're considering partnering with in marriage:

1. Do they love God more than they love you? As flattering as it may be to have someone adore you, it is vital that you not come first in their life. You do not want to be an idol. God will not bless idolatry.

2. Do they have respectful, healthy relationships with their parents and siblings? The way they already do family relationships is what you can expect from them if you start a new family with them. Spend a lot of time with them and their family together so that you can get a good idea of what is in store for you.

3. Do they have the same life mission as you? It will be very hard to accomplish your heart's mission if you are tied to someone who is headed in a different direction than you are.

Once you are married, you have a life time to grow and strategize together in your life mission. Every family should take time to formulate their mission.

What does your family bring to the world to make it a better place?

If you find that you are not headed in the same direction as your spouse, bailing on them is not an option. You will need to find a new mission that you both can invest in.

God is completely committed to helping you have a bright future. He is so faithful to complete the work that He has started in you. It is hard to get off track when you have a sincere desire to follow Him.

He even takes your mistakes and weaves them into your destiny to make your story powerful. He redeems every messy situation to the core.

Think of a wall with a hole knocked into it. God doesn't just slap some scotch tape and spray paint onto it. He does a thorough repair job to the point that the wall looks brand new.

Destiny key: Don't be overwhelmed by trying to figure out God's will for your life. Submit yourself to God and your leaders, get into a place of peace, and do what God is putting in your heart.

For more practical help with relationships, I recommend that you follow Danny Silk.

Lovingonpurpose.com

For I am confident of this
very thing,
that He who began a good work
in you
will perfect it
until the day of Christ Jesus.

Philippians 1:6

Chapter 10

A Call to Motherhood

I settled down easily into married life. Christopher and I both worked at Teen Challenge. He worked as a counselor, and I ran the kitchen. My time with Mercy Ships gave me all of the experience that I needed to run the kitchen for the staff and students.

> When he looked down at the baby he was shocked to see that he was holding a rubber chicken!

Shortly before our second wedding anniversary God gave us our first child, Judah Alexander. It is very common for pregnant women to have crazy dreams, but in our family it was Christopher who had the weirdest pregnancy dream.

Just before Judah was born Christopher had a dream about the birth. The baby was born, and the doctor handed him over for Christopher to hold. When he looked down at the baby he was shocked to see that he was holding a rubber chicken!

Judah and I on our way to Monterrey, Mexico

Happily, Christopher's dream did not come true. Our baby turned out to be human in every way.

He had blond hair and blue eyes and was perfect. We took him on his first mission's trip to Monterrey, Mexico when he was six months old.

Less than two years later Levi Christopher joined us, followed by Elijah James, and Zoe Elizabeth.

I gave birth to four babies in five years.

When Levi was five weeks old we left Tennessee and moved back to Iowa so that Christopher could support his brother Dave, as he had just become the senior pastor of Heartland Church in Ankeny, Iowa.

It was a big move for us. We decided to leave our comfort zone and head out without knowing where we were going to live and work. We knew that God was calling us, so we went.

Thankfully by the time we actually arrived in Iowa, God had sorted everything out for us. God is so good and faithful. He has taken such good care of us.

After a couple of years God made a way for Christopher to be on staff at the church that his brother pastors.

God has opened doors for both of us to travel to the nations. Christopher has been able to travel a lot more than I have over the years. Now that the kids are older, I am getting to travel more.

There is a call on our lives to be a spiritual mother and father to the ones that God highlights to us in all parts of the world.

There are different levels to this. Some people we are meant to walk very closely with through the different stages of their lives over many years. For others we may only give a hug, a smile, or a quick word of encouragement.

> Some people we are meant to walk very closely with through the different stages of their lives over many years. For others we may only give a hug, a smile, or a quick word of encouragement.

I believe that the enemy knows about this call on our lives for parenting. He tried to snuff it out by attacking us fiercely in the area of adoption.

A few years ago our family went through a very difficult season when we experienced a failed adoption. We had a toddler foster son living with us for over six months, and just before the adoption was due to go through, everything fell apart.

That season was one of the hardest times of my life. Parenting that precious boy felt to me like I imagine it would feel to parent a terminally ill child.

To some people that may sound too dramatic or even insensitive to those who have lost biological children. All I can tell you is that is how I felt. There was so much uncertainty.

Uncertainty is very hard for me. I like to "make a plan and work the plan." Hourly we were waiting for word to confirm or deny that this baby would be ours forever. I guess I always had a sinking feeling that things weren't going to go the way we hoped.

> Just before the adoption was due to go through, everything fell apart.

We had been told that this child was going to be ours; it was just a matter of getting the papers signed. The adoption workers told us to bond with him and to get our heads wrapped around the idea that he was our son.

At the last minute they changed their minds and put him into another home. We were heart broken. To make matters worse we were told that one of our references had come back negative. They told us that someone thought we would not be good adoptive parents. This struck at the core of my identity as a mom.

It was like the enemy wanted to convince me that I was not good enough to be a mom to anyone besides my four biological kids. He wanted to keep me from stepping up to mother at all.

It was also very painful to see our kids' hearts break, as they had to let go of their "brother." We had to help them process while we were processing through everything ourselves.

I remember during that season having days where I would literally daydream about escaping. I would imagine how wonderful it would be to just sit all alone in a dark, silent room for hours. It was like there was just too much noise and uncertainty spinning all around me, and I needed peace.

After we got the news that the little guy would be moving on, I spent the next few months just recovering and resting. The grief process just takes some time.

We all had to walk through a process of forgiving and letting the pain go. This looked different and happened on a different timeline for each of us.

Looking back, I can see how much the Lord held us during those devastating moments. He sent some wonderful people into our lives who loved us well when we really needed it.

He brought our spiritual father Bob Phillips into our lives during this time. He helped to comfort our hearts when they were shattered. We had no idea how important this relationship would become.

Though I felt like everything was falling apart, God was actually building strength deep inside of me. Those hard times built perseverance. I cannot say that I lived in perfect peace, but I can say that I fought hard to stay in peace, and it was worth the fight.

> I cannot say that I lived in perfect peace, but I can say that I fought hard to stay in peace, and it was worth the fight.

True peace only comes through Jesus.

Stayed Upon Jehovah,
Hearts are Fully Blest,
Finding as He Promised,
Perfect Peace and Rest.

~ Francis R. Havergal ~

My mom and dad tried to adopt at least two different children over the years, and we tried to adopt this precious one, but it was not to be.

It is okay, because the parenting call is on our family and God is giving us many spiritual sons and daughters all over the world. All of creation is longing for the sons and daughters of God to rise up. Our Father is allowing us to run with Him as we call His children to come up higher.

Strategy to Unlock Your Destiny

The Next Generation Needs YOU

Behold, children are a gift of the Lord, the fruit of the womb is a reward. Like arrows in the hand of a warrior, so are the children of one's youth. How blessed is the man whose quiver is full of them; They will not be ashamed when they speak with their enemies in the gate. (Psalm 127:3-5)

Parenting is the ultimate way to raise up disciples. We're not all called to full time ministry, but we're all called to make disciples and feed our Father's sheep.

It is time to get a vision for the next generation. What will your kids create that will change the world? Whatever it is, they will have a very difficult time accomplishing it without your care and wisdom.

Be intentional in raising your kids. They are your story. Ask Holy Spirit what your child's destiny is. Then take time to get to know your child well. This way you can start to form a strategy to prepare them for their future.

Try to think outside the box in raising your kids. Every child has a unique personality and learning style. It is better to work with their individuality than against it.

It is helpful to think of the parenting journey as raising adults, not taking care of kids. The nurture and training you give out now will affect generations to come. Your kids are your inheritance.

Ask God to bring spiritual kids into your life too. You will know who they are because you will feel affection for them and a desire to see them become all they can be.

Having so fond an affection for you, we were well-pleased to impart to you not only the gospel of God but also our own lives, because you had become very dear to us. (I Thes. 2:8)

Don't force your way into their lives and scare them off. Take time to let a connection develop naturally.

Spiritual kids may be in your life for a season, but what you give to them during that time can build strength in them that will last for the rest of their lives.

Don't be jealous or possessive when God brings other mentors into your kids' lives. We don't own anyone. Any positive influence in our kids' lives should be welcomed with gratitude.

It is very important not to try to take the place of your spiritual child's natural parents. The best thing you can do for them is to help them form the healthiest relationship possible with their biological family.

Make sure to establish good boundaries in spiritual parenting. If you try to work harder on your adult child's life than they are willing to work, you will live in frustration. Without peace you cannot help anyone.

There will be times where you will need to bring correction to your kids. Redirecting them proves they are true sons.

We have to be willing to have tough, awkward conversations in order to move our kids forward in their destiny.

Remember how my dad made the tough choice to postpone my wedding, and Sandra Collier spoke up and told me the truth even when I didn't want to hear it? Those heroic acts are exactly what I'm talking about.

- I want to remind you that **YOU MATTER!**

- The way you walk into a room matters.

- Your presence matters.

- Your smile matters.

- The words that come out of your mouth matter.

You can literally shift the atmosphere around you wherever you go!

- People need you.

- They need what you have to offer.

- They need the wisdom you have gained from your many life experiences.

Destiny key: Put on your peace and joy, so you can show up powerfully. Don't be afraid to show up in other people's lives.

Beth L Olson

Chapter 11

A Family Trip to the Southern Hemisphere

In 2011, seemingly out of nowhere God told us to go to Argentina. We had a guest minister from Argentina speak at our church on a Sunday morning. By the time the service was over Christopher and I both knew without even talking to each other that we were to go.

There was no reason in the natural for us to want to uproot our family and move to the southern hemisphere. God clearly spoke the same thing about us to several people in our church as well, so we decided to submit the idea to our leaders.

God had spoken a word to our spiritual father Bob Phillips that if he would pour into Argentina, God would pour into America. We were to be a part of that. We did not know if we would be going on a short trip, or if we would be moving there forever.

With the help of our leaders, parents, and spiritual fathers we made the decision to take our family to Buenos Aires, Argentina for three months. We would be helping another ministry launch a Bible school.

Christopher and I flew down to Buenos Aires with our spiritual father Bob to check the living situation out. I was willing to just go blindly, but they wanted me to go for a short trip without the kids first.

That was a wise thing to do. I was able to walk through grocery stores to see what kinds of things I would want to pack when we brought the kids. It was nice to be able to get a feel of the city and the culture ahead of time too.

> On Super Bowl Sunday 2012, we headed for the airport with our four kids, twelve suitcases, and six carry-on bags.

On Super Bowl Sunday 2012, we headed for the airport with our four kids, twelve suitcases, and six carry-on bags.

Zoe was the only one of our kids who had ever flown before, and that was when she was a baby. We had to fly to Atlanta, then all night to Chile, layover for 4 hours, and then fly to Buenos Aires.

When we left Iowa there were several inches of snow on the ground. We boarded a plane in the middle of the winter and exited a plane the next day in the middle of the summer. When we walked out of the airport in Argentina the weather was in the nineties.

Judah expressed what we all felt when he said, "Wow, I forgot about sweating." It was such a strange feeling to be so warm.

By the time we arrived at our apartment we had not slept for two days. When you are sleep deprived and in culture shock everything seems surreal.

We had to meet our landlords and sign paperwork on an apartment that we had never seen, before we could be left alone to start to get our heads screwed on right.

A couple of our kids had had enough and started to melt down in front of everyone. I just wanted to get the papers signed and get all of the extra people out of the apartment so that we could start to help our kids adjust.

Christopher just felt bad. He is always the more compassionate parent. I took the stance that kids are resilient, and that they would adjust quickly.

We got unpacked and took a couple days to catch up on sleep. The apartment only had two bedrooms, so every night was party time in the kids' room. The time change meant that we were all awake late into the night and could barely drag ourselves out of bed in the mornings.

The apartment was a safe place to live, but it was nothing fancy. There was a huge window in the living room ceiling that leaked a lot every time it rained. The kids got very used to checking the weather report and moving everything out of the living room if there was a chance of rain.

There were no windows that we could open in the apartment and it was very humid. One time we got caught in a bad storm while we were walking home from the Bible school. We hung our clothes around the apartment to dry, and it took three days before they were done drying.

Life in Buenos Aires was night and day different to life in Ankeny, Iowa. It is very quiet in Ankeny, and we can easily drive to the other side of town in fifteen minutes.

There are thirteen million people in Buenos Aires. We lived right down town in the federal district. Quiet is the very last word I would use to describe it.

We walked or took the subway everywhere we went. At first the ten blocks to the Bible school felt like a very long hike, but before long we were all experts at walking wherever we needed to go.

We had to go to several shops every day to buy our food. We'd go to one shop for meat, one for fruits and vegetables, and another for milk and staples. The six of us would walk down the street each carrying bags of groceries. My appreciation for Wal-Mart and my mini-van grew so much.

> It was not unusual to find someone sleeping on the sidewalk outside of our apartment.

Many times we would head out to the store or laundromat only to find out that it was a public holiday and everything was closed.

I spent the mornings homeschooling the kids. Then we would walk to the Bible school to have lunch with the students. We spent the evenings at the Bible school with the students and other teachers.

When we were not busy with the Bible school, we took time to explore the city. There were homeless people living on the streets everywhere. It was not unusual to find someone sleeping on the sidewalk outside of our apartment.

There were times when our kids would see people digging through trash cans looking for something to eat. We tried to help the ones who we could.

Sometimes Christopher would take Judah and Levi out to the park to talk to homeless people and give them some food. I know that the boys will never forget it.

Elijah, Judah, Zoe, and Levi at EMVIAR Bible School

There was an elderly homeless man who hung out near a park that we used to go to. Christopher became friends with him. He gave the man one of his shirts and some food, and was able to pray for him.

One day when Christopher stopped by to check on him, the man's friends told Christopher that he had had a heart attack and passed away. It was sad. We were so thankful that we had a chance to know him and pray with him.

While we were in Argentina, Granny went home to be with Jesus. She was eighty-three years old. She tripped and fell at her home one day and as a result everything in her body got really complicated. Within three weeks she received her upgrade to heaven.

I am so thankful for modern technology. I was able to talk with Granny by FaceTime to say good-bye a couple of days before she left us.

It was really hard to miss her funeral. I felt that there was no way I could leave Christopher and the kids in the living condition we were in.

There is sacrifice involved in following Jesus. There is a price to be paid, and an offering to be laid on the altar. There cannot be fire without a sacrifice.

> There is a price to be paid, and an offering to be laid on the altar. There cannot be fire without a sacrifice.

After we had been in Buenos Aires for two months, Amy Griffin from our church in Ankeny flew down to join us for our final month. It was strength and joy to have her with us. Working with a team is the way to go as far as I am concerned. There is a reason that Jesus sent His disciples out two by two.

Our family touched many lives while we were in Argentina, but more than anything God did deep things in our own hearts. We all came back different.

Identity was solidified in us, and the adventures we shared pulled us closer together as a family unit.

Christopher, Judah, Levi, Elijah, Zoe, & Beth

Strategy to Unlock Your Destiny

Unpacking Your Bags

Have you ever been betrayed? In order to be betrayed you have to have loved and trusted someone deeply.

It is stunning to me that Jesus knew from the beginning that Judas would betray Him, but it did not hold Him back from including Judas in His inner circle and risking His heart.

I think that if I knew ahead of time that someone was going to betray me, I would not even introduce myself much less bring the person into my inner circle.

Jesus is so different from me. He blows my mind. He keeps His love turned on towards all people 100% of the time.

For Jesus knew from the beginning who they were who did not believe, and who it was that would betray Him. John 6:64b

Jesus' life clearly illustrates this truth: even if you do everything absolutely perfectly, you will still experience rejection.

Perfection does not equal acceptance from the people around you. You might even say that the more Christ like you become, the more you may experience rejection.

Jesus walked in confidence because His sense of self-worth did not come from His companions.

When the Jews wanted to kill Him He said, *"Truly, truly, I say to you, the Son can do nothing of Himself, unless it is something He sees the Father doing; for whatever the Father does, these things the Son also does in like manner. For the Father loves the Son, and shows Him all things that He Himself is doing.* John 5:19-20

Jesus' identity was completed wrapped up in what the Father thought about Him and in living according to His Father's wishes.

You won't be healed of your rejection by analyzing the source of your rejection but by looking at the source of your acceptance. -Bob Sorge

Your Father loves you with the same exact love He loves Jesus with. Make living your life in Him your highest aim, and the acceptance or rejection from people will lose its hold on you.

Destiny key: Any pain you have stored up in your heart from betrayal belongs to you. You can choose to own it and to let it go. Choose to let it go

today. You don't have to live in bondage for even one more day.

O God of burning, cleansing flame,
Send the fire

Your blood - bought gift today we claim,
Send the fire today

God of Elijah, hear our cry,
Send the fire

And make us fit to live or die,
send the fire today

To burn up every trace of sin,
to bring the light and glory in
The revolution now begins,
Send the fire today

It's fire we want, for fire we plead,
Send the fire

The fire will meet our every need,
Send the fire today

Give us strength to always do what's right,
And grace to conquer in the fight
for power to walk this world in white,
Send the fire today

Look down and see this waiting host
And send the promised Holy Ghost
We need another Pentecost,
Send the fire today

To make our weak hearts strong and brave,
Send the fire

To live a dying world to save,
Send the fire

See us on Your altar lay,
Send the fire

We give our lives to You today,
Send the fire

(Original lyrics by William Booth. Adapted by Lindell Cooley.)

Beth L Olson

Chapter 12

What Brand Are You?

As children we tend to absorb labels. Our parents should be the ones who brand us with good words, calling us up into our destinies. In many cases our parents carried negative labels themselves and had no clue how to brand us or that it was even part of their job description.

Some common labels are:

- Scatterbrained

- Shy

- Dumb

- Lazy

- Below average

- Dramatic

- Stubborn

- Clumsy

- Accident prone

Maybe a doctor or other "professional" labeled you with:

- ADHD

- DID

- PTSD

- Some other series of letters

These labels do not have the power to define you forever unless you let them. You can move beyond your childhood and be a powerful adult.

When I was a child, I used to speak like a child, think like a child, reason like a child; when I became a man, I did away with childish things. (1 Corinthians 13:11)

You were a child then. You are not now. You are an adult. You really can throw off all of those old labels from when you were a child and embrace new labels.

You have what it takes to be:

- Powerful

- Mature

- Wise

- Peaceful

- Friendly

Maybe you do not have any earthly parents who are able to bless you in this, but you have generations of ancestors cheering you on!

Therefore, since we have so great a cloud of witnesses surrounding us, let us also lay aside every encumbrance and the sin which so easily entangles us, and let us run with endurance the race that is set before us. (Hebrews 12:1 NASB)

Take some time to think about who you need to be in order to do what you want to do with your life. If the idea you come up with seems comfortable then it is not big enough. It should feel like something you cannot do on your own.

Ask Holy Spirit to tell you what Father God says about who He thinks you are and how He feels about you.

The combination of these things will help you figure out which direction to head.

Put it into one sentence, then put it into your reminders in your phone and set the alarm to go off at a certain time each day. Read it out loud every day. Do it until it feels true and natural.

When I was a child I was very quiet. People around me started to call me shy. I latched onto that label and shrunk more and more inside myself. This was another strategy of the enemy to keep me from my mothering role.

One sentence I put into my phone for many months was, "I am a powerful, outspoken mother to nations." In order to bless people around me, I had to reprogram myself to open my mouth with confidence.

Do not conform to the pattern of this world, but be transformed by the renewing of your mind. Then you will be able to test and approve what God's will is--His good, pleasing and perfect will. (Romans 12:2 NIV)

In order to follow God's will for your life and fulfill your destiny, you will have to work with Holy Spirit to have your mind renewed.

Destiny key: You do not have to be who you have always been! You are free to be a whole new person.

Don't let your dreams just be dreams. Start to make your thinking and therefore behavior align with God's value system instead of the enemy's.

Maybe you lack the confidence that you will be successful. You really have to start somewhere though.

Remember, pride is sometimes what stops us from trying. None of us likes to look silly in front of other people, but you simply cannot be perfect at something the first time you do it. You have to be willing to try and to fail. Fear of looking like a fool is pride.

God is opposed to the proud, but gives grace to the humble. (James 4:6)

Everything worth doing is worth doing poorly….in the beginning.

You have to start somewhere. You have to get right up to the starting line and take that first step. No one is born knowing how to walk gracefully. You literally have to take baby steps.

Epilogue

When I was a little girl living on the mission field we used to sing a scripture song based on Psalm 2:8.

Ask of Me, and I will surely give the nations as Your inheritance, and the very ends of the earth as Your possession.

We do not always realize that the prayers we pray and the songs we sing really do get answered. Even today God is answering our residual prayers from years past.

God is making our family and our church a breakthrough to the nations, and He wants YOU to get in on it too!

Ask of Me, and I will give the nations
As an inheritance for you,
As an inheritance for you,
My children

Ask of Me, and I will give the nations
As an inheritance for you,
Ask of Me.

Here am I, send me to the nations
As an ambassador for You,
As an ambassador for You,
My Father

Here am I, send me to the nations
As an ambassador for You,
Here am I

(Bob Kilpatrick)

P.S.

There is only one way to have true peace, and that is through Jesus Christ. We cannot live life to its fullest apart from God.

If you say that Jesus is God's Son and believe in your heart that God raised Him from the dead, you will be saved from hell and spend eternity with God in heaven. This however does not guarantee that you will live in peace before you die.

I believe that if you want to live life with the most amount of peace possible, you have to surrender every part of your life to God.

Maybe God won't ask you to sell everything and move to another country, but He might. Position your heart continually to be ready to do anything He asks.

Don't just be a fan of Jesus. Be completely His. Give Him every part of you. This is the pathway to true peace and joy!

Beth L Olson

Websites
To Move You
Forward in
Your Destiny

My site: bethlolson.com

My husband, Christopher Olson:
facebook.com/christopherolson

My mom, Leanne Goff: leannegoffministries.org

Heartland Church: heartlandchurchonline.com

Julaine Christensen: currentfireministries.com

YWAM Mercy Ships: mercyships.org

Practical help for raising creative kids:
firefliesaglow.com

Danny Silk: lovingonpurpose.com

Leif Hetland: globalmissionawareness.com

Made in the USA
Charleston, SC
25 August 2016